Anthony Smith, well known for his books on zoo-life, ballooning and expeditions, is also frequently heard on BBC radio taking a 'sideways look at life'. In this collection of the best of his broadcasts, he casts a quizzical eye on a wide variety of subjects including dogs, the countryside and the family 'Smith'. Always fresh and observant, Anthony Smith makes us take a new look at issues, topics and everyday happenings that we tend to take for granted.

A SIDEWAYS LOOK

ANTHONY SMITH

London
UNWIN PAPERBACKS
Boston   Sydney

First published by Unwin Paperbacks 1983

UNWIN ® PAPERBACKS
40 Museum Street, London WC1A 1LU, UK

Unwin Paperbacks
Park Lane, Hemel Hempstead, Herts HP2 4TE, UK

George Allen & Unwin Australia Pty Ltd
8 Napier Street, North Sydney, NSW 2060, Australia

British Library Cataloguing in Publication Data

Smith, Anthony, 1926–
  A sideways look.
I. Title
828′.91407   PR6069.M
ISBN 0-04-808037-3

Set in 10 on 11 point Century Schoolbook
by V & M Graphics Ltd, Aylesbury, Bucks
and printed in Great Britain
by Guernsey Press Co. Ltd, Guernsey, Channel Islands

Acknowledgements

These pieces are based on radio broadcasts given in the author's radio series *A Sideways Look* for the BBC.

They were first broadcast as follows:

British Genius (24 May 1977); *Smoking* (8 June 1977); *Safety* (21 November 1977); *Age* (10 April 1978); *Women* (1 May 1978); *Athletics* (8 May 1978); *Talking to Strangers* (15 May 1978); *Life and Limb* (22 May 1978); *English* (29 May 1978); *Notice-Boards* (5 June 1978); *Steele's Road Decoded* (9 October 1978); *Fire Precautions* (23 October 1978); *Committees* (6 November 1978); *Christmas* (29 May 1979); *Time Zones* (19 June 1979); *Travel Rights* (26 June 1979); *Names* (4 August 1979); *Godparents* (7 July 1979); *Eating Meat* (14 July 1979); *Japanese Road Deaths* (9 January 1980); *Cancer* (30 January 1980); *Bicycles* (6 February 1980); *Puberty* (23 July 1980); *Rabies* (6 August 1980); *The Smith Family* (7 September 1980); *Dogs* (5 March 1981); *A Nun* (19 March 1981); *Suicide* (26 March 1981); *Nuclear War* (23 April 1981)

As all these talks have been broadcast by the BBC I wish to express thanks to that organisation for permitting me to air my views, and in particular to David Paterson. He not only coined their Sideways name but believed that an individual, novel and researched point of view could add to the normal range of broadcasting. Two protagonists repeating age-old arguments might create balance, but a Sideways look could, he suggested, be more refreshing from time to time. My thanks therefore to him, and to Michael Bright, Geoff Deehan, David Perry, and Alison Richards, other BBC producers who helped the programmes on to the air with advice, encouragement, and enthusiasm.

A. S.

Contents

British Genius

I remember hearing of a man who was uncannily accurate in assessing the value of inventions set before him. His reputation was founded upon the fact that he was right on 99.9 per cent of occasions. So I enquired further about this man as I could not understand such perspicacity. And then I learned that he had but one simple rule. He looked at the inventions; he studied them; he seemed to give great thought to each and every one. And then, with the simplicity of his golden rule, he rejected all of them. Every single one. No invention of any kind received his blessing. Consequently, he *was* 99.9 per cent right and he only failed with .1 per cent, the proportion of inventions that are worthwhile.

Looking back over our technological history, with all the advantages of years of hindsight, the very few good inventions seem so obvious. Of course the wheel was a good idea, and weights and measures, and the clock and the calendar, and a means of recording one's measurements. Anyone could think of them. But, come to think of it, not a single European did so first. They were all dreamed up by other people in other places.

I say all this because this is Inventions Week. On Friday the British Genius Exhibition opens in Battersea Park, London. In no uncertain manner it is promoting the inventive ability of the British in the past 100 years, in the present and, more speculatively, in the future. Undeniably, the list is impressive. It ranges from DNA and cats' eyes to the tank and the tin-hat, from penicillin and the jet engine to the heart-lung machine and float glass. As they said at a press conference to mark the exhibition: British Genius is alive and well. Of course, as we also all know only too well, Britain possibly leads the world in inventing things and then not following them up. But, as this is not 'Knocking Britain Week' I'll slide over that one and get back to the inventions themselves. What kind of person is an inventor?

Do particular countries shine at inventing things? And do
we only remember as inventions those things which have
been thought of first by our fellow countrymen? Say the
word 'Invention' at an Englishman and the chances are
that he will say Radar or Davy's Safety Lamp or Terylene
back at you. I suppose any nation has a tendency to
promote its own citizens and their achievements, and there
is the apocryphal story that, according to Russians and
Russian textbooks, the Russians invented virtually everything. I am sure they don't go *quite* as far as that, but every
country is a bit myopic, and so are we.

For instance, as I sit at my desk, there is a typewriter
straight ahead of me. There is a light bulb directly overhead, a tape recorder to one side, a camera nearby
containing colour film, a ballpoint pen, a piece of photo-
copied paper, an umbrella, scissors, a hinge, a safety pin, a
pot made on a wheel, spectacles, a firework – yes, it's a fairly
confusing study – a compass, some loom-made cloth, a
book, a transistor radio, a zip fastener, a balloon – well, a
picture of one – a telephone, a microscope, a pencil, a can-
opener, nylon, a safety razor, a record player, a record, a
non-stick frying pan, and that's enough for the time being,
but not one of those things was invented by 'British
Genius'. Because I don't happen to possess a hovercraft in
that room, or a miner's safety lamp, or a Whittle jet engine,
it's suddenly quite easy to get the impression – from a
roomful of stuff – that Britons haven't invented anything.
It's a wrong impression, of course, but that list does show
how many entirely familar objects both had to be invented
and, as it happens, were invented by people of other
nations.

Besides, just how many of my desk's inventions could we
put a name or even a country to? Well, the typewriter was
American and largely the work of Christopher Sholes. Who,
say the rest of us? The ballpoint pen was invented by two
Hungarians, named Biro, then living in Argentina. It was
Valdemar Poulsen, a Dane, who was the father of magnetic
recording – the tape recorder. The safety razor was the work
of King Camp Gillette – quite a name, and an American.
The balloon was French. The zip was invented by an
American, but it was a Swede – Gideon Sundback – who in

1913 made it work reliably. (Well, fairly reliably. To my mind, it only rates as a half-invention.) The phonograph was, of course, the work of Thomas Alva Edison, the American who filed more than a thousand patents which contributed to incandescent light, the storage and generation of electricity, the movies and so on. Photo-copying – or Xerography – was the work of Chester Carlson of Seattle. The telephone, although much improved by Edison, was invented by Alexander Graham Bell, born a Scot but an emigrant to the New World by the time of his discovery. Nylon was American, at the Du Pont Laboratories. The pencil – graphite set in wood – was first made by Konrad Gesner in Germany. And on and on. All could have been made in Britain, but weren't.

What is necessary for an invention is not only the wit to stumble upon the discovery, but also the shove, the drive, the fanaticism crucial to make others realise that something new and exciting has arrived. Read of any invention and the original spark of an idea is then – almost – put out by the dampness emanating from those who should have known better. Gillette, for instance, knew he was on to a winner with his notion of a cheap disposable blade, but he knew nothing about steel and learned very quickly that the steel men saw no future in his idea. Eventually he had to go round the corner, so to speak, and get a lamp manufacturer to help him out. Richard Trevithick, one of the two men credited with the high-pressure steam engine, not only had to overcome the practical problems inherent in his idea but also the tremendous opposition of James Watt, the steam engine pioneer who should certainly have known better. Watt said that Trevithick deserved hanging – no less – for introducing the high-pressure engine. The history of invention is full of what could be called disinvention, the ability to resist whenever anyone suggests anything new. In 1906 the Engineering Editor of *The Times* said that 'all attempts at artificial aviation ... are not only dangerous to human life but foredoomed to failure from an engineering point of view'. In 1910, seven years after the Wright brothers had first flown and four years before the First World War, the British Secretary of State for War said: 'We do not consider that aeroplanes will be of any possible use for war purposes'. Later on, and in 1939, Winston Churchill said that 'atomic energy might be as good as our present-day explosives, but it is unlikely to produce anything very much more dangerous'.

Perhaps it is only reasonable to expect that journalists and politicians can get it wrong. But Heinrich Hertz, the German physicist who discovered radio waves, didn't think they would have any practical application. Robert A. Millikan, who was the first man to realise the charge on an electron, and who, therefore, knew a thing or two about the atom, wrote in 1930 that 'There is no appreciable energy available to man through atomic disintegration'. The great Lord Rutherford, known as the founder of modern atomic theory, didn't believe even at the time of his death (in 1937) that nuclear energy would ever be used on a large scale. So, if he got it wrong, small wonder that Winston Churchill was getting it wrong two years later.

The story of the jet engine is one of the great sagas of invention and one of the most illuminating. We all know that a great interval of time elapsed between its invention and its application; but if it's any comfort, other countries, such as Germany, didn't do much better. Sir Frank Whittle hit upon the idea of combining a gas turbine with jet propulsion in 1929. Unknown to him, and – one assumes – unknown to the French aviation industry for they certainly did nothing about it, an engine similar to Whittle's had been patented nine years earlier by a Frenchman named Guillaume. Anyway, Whittle patented his idea, tried to interest both the Air Ministry and the aero-engineering firms, failed everywhere, and was so discouraged that he let his patent lapse in 1935. However, he continued to work on the idea, and managed to get the small amount of money necessary from the investment bankers, O.T. Falk. The Air Ministry, Whittle's employers, then allowed him to work for six hours a week with the company named Power Jets Limited which was financed by Falk. Only in 1937 did they let him work full time on the engine, and only the following year did they step in with some money.

Over in Germany they were doing better, but not all that better. Hans von Ohain patented his turbo-jet in 1934, and was taken on by Heinkel, the aircraft manufacturers. But

the Heinkel engineers were unenthusiastic. Simultaneously, and unknown to Heinkel, the rival Junkers Aircraft
Company were also working on turbines. When Junkers
and Heinkel applied to the German Air Ministry for
financial assistance, they were both turned down with
the argument that the companies themselves should
finance such work. It was not until the European war had
started that German Government money became available
for the jet engine. So Britain at least got Government
money first, but the Germans won the race when the
Messerschmitt 262 fighter went into service in late 1944.

So, there were parallel inventiveness and parallel frustration. But it's particularly interesting that both sets of
inventors were people either quite unconnected with the
aircraft industry or, if they were connected, who had
worked on the airframe side of things and not on the engine
side. Time and again, this is the pattern. An outsider comes
along and, eventually, after an uphill struggle, revolu-
tionises an industry. Kodachrome, for instance, was the
work of two independent inventors, both students of music,
who - by 1923 - had managed to get a crude picture on a
single film containing all the colours. They were then taken
up by private backers and Eastman Kodak. Radio had its
foundations in science, but the subsequent inventions
based on this accumulated theory were carried out by
individual inventors who had nothing to do with the
communications business. Such big firms only joined in
when the usefulness of the invention had been firmly
established. Dr Johnson, as usual, had summed it up all
those years before. 'Is not a Patron, my Lord, one who looks
with unconcern on a man struggling for life in the water, and,
when he has reached ground, encumbers him with help?'
Had Samuel Johnson spent more time among inventors he
might have been harsher still. Is not a patron one who
pushes the swimmer back into the water, time and again,
until he comes up with the answer?

The big trouble with inventions, I suppose, is not so much
the original idea - and judging by the tens of thousands of
ideas patented every year we, as a race, are not short of
inventiveness - but the cost of putting that idea into
practice. We say, happily, that if you build a better mouse-

trap the world will beat a path to your door. There is something very simple and cheap-sounding about a new mouse-trap, but most inventions are not like that. No one beat a path to Alexander Fleming's laboratory when, in 1928, he discovered that a penicillium mould killed bacteria. In fact, from 1932 to 1939 no work on the development of penicillin was done at all. When war produced the necessary stimulus, and when the need was suddenly imperative for such an effective antibiotic, the development got going but cost millions. Most invention is not of mouse-traps and tin-openers, but of bigger and more expensive items. Some quoted figures are $6 million for the development of nylon and £4 million for Terylene. Much earlier, and when the Victorians were busy arguing about the Patent Law, Bessemer said that he had spent £16,000 on his steel process. Charles Goodyear spent $130,000 in finding a commercial process that could use his new technique of vulcanising rubber. Sir Charles Parsons spent £100,000 in developing the steam turbine. Much later, EMI reported that it spent £550,000 on research and development of television, and the cost of developing the long-playing record has been put at $250,000. These may seem small sums when we know how much steel, rubber, turbine power, television, and how many LPs are produced today, but the developers weren't to know that then. If an invention is really something quite new, not only are people getting on without it anyway, but there is an established industry quite unprepared for its advance. And often unwilling to contemplate such a major change, let alone finance it.

It is argued, of course, that without the protection of the Patent Law no one would bother to go ahead with development cost. It's risky enough making something new, without the extra threat that someone else could cream off all the profits as soon as the development had been concluded. But there used to be quite a strong lobby against patents. Isambard Kingdom Brunel, for example, and Sir William Armstrong, another engineer, argued that all inventions were merely improvements or adaptations of existing knowledge. They said that the business of invention had become a social process, in which the contribution of no one individual could be crucial. It's a thought to ponder on. Would inventions be put into use more speedily if there were not the Patent Law enabling a few to take advantage of each new spark of thought? And do we want that speediness? What's wrong with the mouse-trap of today?

Anyway, as I said, this is Inventions Week because the British Genius Exhibition opens at Battersea Park, London. It will, so they say, be a rallying point in this year of 1977 for wholly justifiable national pride, and they hope that a million of us will beat a path to see all those better mouse-traps of every kind that we have dreamed up within a century.

Smoking

The other day I bumped into a medical friend who'd obviously had a bad day.

'What a waste of time,' he said. 'Why did I spend all those years training to be a doctor when I should have learned something completely different? I should have learned *not* how to cure people of disease but how to stop them doing their level best to get that disease. If I'm going to do any good I've got to stop people doing themselves harm. That's all. It's as simple as that.'

Together we then watched a ten-year-old light a cigarette. My medical friend snorted, threw up his hands, kicked at a handy cigarette carton, and was off.

I've always felt that the Government's enthusiasm to stop us smoking cigarettes, despite the so-called new offensive, has about as much shove behind it as, say, a schoolboy's enthusiasm to ask for more homework. Besides, the rest of us have learned to distrust Governments even before we have our first cigarette. We say that they do all right out of it, so why should they care. We say they get the tax and no wonder they don't really want us to stop smoking. They must make millions. And we are right, in a way. In the year 1975/76 the tax received on cigarettes alone was just short of £1,680 million. Of course that's a lot of money, even for these days, but it's only £30 a year on average from every one of us. I think there's an even better reason for us to go on smoking from the Government's point of view. Even greater quantities of money are involved.

But first to some basic facts about smoking. Those who try to discourage us tell us in general terms about this particular pleasure, about the lung cancer we're far more likely to get if we smoke, about the heart disease we will suffer, about the bronchitis. In slightly more specific terms they say that smoking causes 100,000 premature deaths a year. If that kind of fact doesn't worry us, and sounds rather like another cyclone in Bangladesh, the discouragers try to be more personal. They say that a man – or a woman – who dies early because of smoking has willingly chopped off an average of ten years from his or her life. If a man or woman should by rights have ended their life at 75 they will, because of the cigarette, end at 65 instead. Or, to put it another way round, each cigarette knocks off about seven minutes of life. As a cigarette takes about seven minutes to smoke that means the pleasure is neatly exacting an appropriate toll. Smoke for seven minutes and you'll die seven minutes earlier. Smoke a packet of twenty and over two hours have gone from the other end.

Of course, that's only on average. Like the soldier comforting himself on going into battle, it's the others who'll get the bullets, not him. The general sees the matter rather differently. He knows there will be loss, perhaps 10 per cent, perhaps more, and he plans accordingly. So do Governments. And this is where the smoking battle becomes more significant. It isn't just a matter of tax. It's the fact that cigarettes kill people. It doesn't matter which people, but it does matter that – so long as the smoking habit continues – the average age of death in this country will be about two years less for men. If someone were to wave a wand, and we were all to stop smoking, we'd all, on average, get those two extra years of life. And that would be a terrifying blow to the Government. Quite suddenly, assuming we kicked the habit overnight, the Government would have to find pensions for two more years for each of us. And that would be an enormous whack of money – two more years for every man and woman who reaches retiring age.

Currently the pensions bill is £3,661 million. Even if nothing is done we're going to have twice as many people over sixty-five by the end of the century as we have now. So the pension bill is going to double anyway, and is going to have to be supported by a relatively smaller workforce. There's a fearful lot of pension trouble on its way without adding to the problem by having people living longer.

Let's take the life of one particular individual, someone who proves to be ideal from the Government's point of

view. He's born healthy, but right from the start he builds
up a financial debt to society because - at the beginning -
he is a parasite. His mother stops work to look after him.
He causes child allowances. He gets free medical treatment, and he eats. He then goes to school and builds up the
debt even more. By the time he's ready to work, the State
has paid out quite a bit, and it's high time he started to pay
it back. So he works, and pays his taxes. By the time he's,
say, thirty, he's perhaps paid back all that he was
originally given in the form of tax rebates, orange-juice,
school-books, teachers and subsidised existence. After
thirty, or more or less, he begins building up a credit. The
State is glad to have him around. He's a tax-payer, and
he's productive. When the time comes for him to retire, the
State will feel that it owes him a decent retirement. But,
supposing he dies on the very day that he leaves the
factory for the very last time, there'll be no pension. It's
sad for him, and for all of us who knew him, but
the State is relieved. There may be a widow, but there's
undeniably less for the State to have to pay.

Now if he's a smoker he's more likely to keel over on his
retirement day *and* will have paid all those extra taxes
during his life time. It was good that he did that, and paid
£100 a year or so for the tax side of his cigarettes, but it's
much more important if his cigarette habit kills him off
prematurely. He will then have opted out of ten years of life,
of ten years of pensions, of ten years - from the State's point
of view - of being a parasite again. But an old person is far
more of a cost to the State than is a baby. Education is a
big bill, but virtually all the expense in bringing up a child
in our society is borne by the parents. The tax relief is just
a sop. The trouble with old people is that they not only get
the pensions but they fill up the hospitals. Half the
hospital beds are currently occupied by people over 65.
And it costs far more for someone to be in hospital than, at
the other end, for someone to be at school. Most old
people aren't in hospital because they're dying. They're
there because old people get sick more often and because
they take longer to get over each mishap. So, if we're going
to have more old people around, which is inevitable in the
next few decades, we're going to have more of them in

hospital, again not dying, just being there. So the hospital bill, already huge, is bound to get bigger. And that pensions bill, almost as huge, is also going to get bigger. And all of this will have to be maintained by a smaller proportion of working people.

So let's take yet another look at the cigarette. And, while we're about it, at drink. And, come to that, at our habit for sitting around, for carrying so much fat upon our person. As we all know only too well, none of these pleasures do us any good. If we didn't drink a lot, and smoke a lot, and overeat, we'd all be physically healthier and we'd all live longer. I've just been reading a realistic Canadian document on the health of Canadians, and what should be done to better it. The conclusion is that 'past improvement has been due mainly to modification of behaviour and changes in the environment, and it is to these *same* influences that we must look particularly for further advance'. In other words, it isn't new drugs that are going to work wonders; we have to work the wonders upon ourselves. Improve our environment and improve our styles of life.

So, does the Government know what would happen if we stopped smoking? And is it worried? Well, I think so, certainly after reading a report called *Smoking and Health* published by our own Department of Health and Social Security. It discusses all the basics of the problem: who gets what disease; and how much these figures would be reduced if, say, 20 per cent of us stopped smoking. But it gets nearer to the really powerful point when it says that 'the assumed reductions in smoking would reduce some health care and social security costs, but other costs would be increased because the increased population would require more services and benefits, particularly in old age'. That's more like it, 'particularly in old age'. But its final sentence gives up such clarity because, I believe, its implications are too worrying not to be obscured in the mists of gobbledygook writing. It says: 'The substantial increase in the total of pensions payments would represent in real resource terms a charge upon the higher level of gross productive potential that may be attained'. In other words, as I see it – and I've read it again and again

– there would be some benefit in having people stop smoking, in that the gross productive potential would go up, but the extra pensions would represent a charge upon it in real resource terms, i.e. they would cost more than the gain. They certainly would. They'd cost thousands of millions of pounds more.

Just suppose that the Government really wanted us to stop. What could it do? Ban all advertising? Or have only those advertisements that were really discouraging, such as a picture of the inside of a cancerous lung? Or spend real money attacking the habit; far, far more than the modest figure currently consumed? But it can't really, not just like that. The revenue is one thing. The prospect of us all living for two more years is another. Both have terrifying financial implications.

I called my dour medical friend, the one who'd set me thinking along these lines, the one who bemoaned that his days should be spent attempting to put right the harm that people were equally busily doing themselves.

'Oh, it's easy,' he said. 'They're not going to give up smoking, no Government either could or would stop them. What you and I have got to do is to stop our *friends* smoking. We *don't* want *them* to die prematurely, but we *do* want as much pension as we can get for ourselves. If everybody else dies, there's going to be more in the kitty for us and our friends.'

So, smoke away the rest of you. Pay your tax on every packet. Knock off seven minutes each time you light up and then you mightn't be around at pension time. But all you *friends* of mine, who puff smoke whenever we meet, who blow it over my food, who pile ash all over my floor, please give it up. Thank you.

Safety

Let's suppose there is some awful accident. We are all shocked, and some of us come out with phrases like 'No expense must be spared to prevent this happening again', 'In future this must be absolutely safe', 'There can be no compromise with safety', and so on. A village child, perhaps, has been crushed by some juggernaut, and there is an immediate outcry for a bypass, a new road that would prevent the repetition of this particular tragedy. The outcry tends to be greater if there is extra cause, in human terms, for a more emotional response. Perhaps the child was one-legged and therefore more vulnerable. Or there is an exceptionally attractive photograph released to the papers. All such facts increase the cry for that new road. Mothers with prams will parade at the accident site. And before long the local councillors will find themselves getting approval for the bypass. All of a sudden, there will be £3 million or so available to 'prevent such a tragedy happening again'. But, putting the bypass accident in a cruder manner, the building of that expensive road means that a value has been put on that one victim's life, namely £3 million. All of a sudden, people being denied kidney machines, for want of a hundred thousand pounds or less, and dying as a consequence, could wonder in their final moments if that £3 million might not have been better spent on them.

Ah, but it doesn't happen like that, does it? Three million pounds for one bypass for one death? I believe it does happen, in varying ways, again and again. Take aircraft crashes. They are, in general, so horrific that we'll demand more and more money to be spent to make them less and less likely. The more and more money doesn't necessarily make everything safer, but we seem to like it being spent, just in case. It's the bypass story, but far more so. With aircraft, and all their sophisticated (which means expensive) back-up equipment, any major change is going to run into hundreds of millions of pounds, and more equipment.

Take the last three really big smashes, in terms of people getting killed. There was the DC10 outside Paris, the collision over Zagreb and the collision on the Tenerife runway. Admittedly there is more than one contributing factor in any accident, and a smokescreen of facts is put about after each one, but essentially there was human error in every one of them. The DC10 had a bad cabin door that should have been changed but wasn't. The Zagreb mid-air encounter was blamed on traffic control. The Jumbos at Tenerife are still being debated but plainly people were at fault. After each accident there was a cry that more money should be spent, a better check system for things like doors, a better computer network (and a figure of £500 million was mentioned) to deter people from slamming aircraft into each other, and better ground radar and better airfields so that aircraft taking off can never hit those still taxying to the take-off point. To stop the possibility of these three kinds of crash ever occurring again would inevitably cost hundreds and hundreds of millions of pounds. Which, like building a bypass, is putting a price on human life. Some lives are being saved at a cost of a few million pounds a life.

An important point about air travel is that it is already very safe. Millions of people travel for millions of miles – and get away with it. As for the motor car or even the home – these are both extraordinarily dangerous, but their accidents are less dramatic. If 500 people all fell at once off step-ladders something might be done about them, but they don't and we still have step-ladders. If we really wanted to save life we could spend a couple of hundred million pounds on each of the major causes of accidents in the home, and get a better deal for our money than if we spent the same amount of cash in trying to make air travel a fraction safer.

The point therefore arises: should we put a firm price on human life? If this piece of equipment costs a million pounds, and is expected to save one life, we are already doing so and are reckoning that a life is worth a million. But, if it is worth a million, then shouldn't we be economical and bring in safety devices that could save, say,

10 lives for a million pounds? Gerald Leach, in a book called *The Biocrats*, once calculated what a million pounds might save. If it were applied to tractor crash-canopies it would save 10 lives, to kidney machines it would give 105 people another five years of life, to cervical cancer screening it would save 720, to lung-cancer X-rays for old smokers it would save 2,400 and so on. His figures may not be right, and all would be disputed, but he is absolutely and indisputably right in his assertion that a million pounds spent in one direction could save far more lives than if spent on some other allegedly life-saving enterprise.

Philip Wills, the glider pilot, wrote a nice story in his book *Free as a Bird* about the safety of some small meteorological rockets. Apparently, these were to be fired westwards from a Scottish island and, after instruments had been ejected to fall to earth by parachute, the rest of the rocket would fall into the Atlantic. Ha ha, said somebody. What happens if these bits fall onto a passing ship? And what happens if someone is walking on that ship just at the very point where the rocket debris falls? Well, there are not too many ships on the ocean, and west of the Hebrides is not a very crowded bit of ocean, but there was risk of hitting a ship, calculated to be about 10 to the power of minus 8. In other words, if there were a hundred firings a year, there would only be one hit in a million years. Of course, it might be next week, but in all probability there would never be a hit in all our lifetimes. And, even if there was, the chances are it would bounce off the deck and not land on the head of some unfortunate sailor. Therefore, the firing of the rockets was safe enough. But apparently not. Someone decided that no firing should take place until the relevant area had been searched by plane. But the chances of accident on a plane journey were far greater – Wills says 1 in 300,000 – than the chances of accident from the dead rocket – 1 in 100 million. In other words, some airmen were put at far greater risk than the sailors they were protecting.

My feeling is that we do this all the time, and would be more rational if we did put a price on human life. So, how about air travel, and should we adopt a different policy?

The other day in a foreign capital I had a nightmare drive
in a fearful taxi heading for an airport while a thousand
other taxis, equally scarred from earlier encounters, took a
thousand other passengers just as scared as I was along
that self-same route. I witnessed several actual hits but we
did not stop. In fact, we had driven with such haste that I
then had ample time to watch the aircraft going about
their business. Competent-looking crew suavely strolled
on board – so different from my sweat-stained driver who
had instilled such fear. The aircraft were being checked
and re-checked. No plane moved anywhere without asking
for permission. They lumbered off at great intervals of
time and in vast acres of space, so different from the
merry-go-roundabouts I had just experienced. Plainly, I
had come nearer to death in the previous half-hour than I
ever would in the next half-dozen hours as my Jumbo
thundered through the sky. If I had £500 million to spare I
decided there and then not to waste it on some refinement of
a refinement to do with air control, but on giving every
taxi in the world those fenders that they have on dodgem
cars. Taxis still wouldn't be as safe as aeroplanes, but I
might have redressed the balance just a little bit.

It is this lack of balance that is so bizarre. We move from
one situation where the chances of dying are, say, 1 in
50,000 to another where the chances are 1 in 500 million. In
that same airport lounge where I pondered upon this
unevenness I knew that the roof had once caved in to kill
dozens of waiting passengers. Someone had apparently
forgotten just how heavy snow can be, and one snow-
storm plus a miscalculation had caused the accident. I do
not know if there has ever been a fatal aircraft accident at
that airport, but I do find it intriguing that the mere
lounge, the terminal lounge, had proved so dangerous.
Presumably, the tragedy could have been avoided by a
very modest expenditure of money. Or by sending up a
dozen men with shovels when the snow began to fall.

Finally, what kind of life is being saved, an old one near
the end of its time, or a young one, or a baby? Doctors have
such thoughts when there is only one kidney machine and
several applicants. The old are old, the babies are
replaceable as like as not within a year or two, but the

youngsters fresh from school would be the greatest loss
from almost every point of view. So it is not quite good
enough saying that this expenditure of a million pounds
will save one life. Is it saving one young life, as in the
prevention of motorcycle accidents, or one old life as in
better fire precautions for an old people's home?

But we don't really like putting such a price on our
various persons, and on equating money with the saving of
life. 'No expense must be spared,' we cry, 'to prevent this
terrible accident happening again.' 'Money must be found
to build this bypass, to have this radar network.' The
trouble is that money is not unlimited. We have to spend it
wisely and get good value for our pounds, even in stopping
accidents. The only yardstick we can apply is: how many
pounds should be spent to save one life? In other words,
how much are we worth? What is the value of a human?

Age

Of all the bureaucratic conveniences, I suppose the one that affects us most is that relating to age. We may be born at 4 lbs or we may be born at 12 lbs; but, despite such disparity, the day when we each decide to leave the uterus is thereafter an immutable part of us. It fixes everything, when we can do this, do that. No one thinks that new-born babies are equal, either in weight, or ability, or maturity, but they are all equal in having their particular birth-date etched forever on the progress of their lives. We go to school at 5, can withdraw money from Post Office Savings at 7, can be convicted of a criminal offence at 10, and so on for the rest of our days.

I know we celebrate birthdays, and they are fun things to have, but my query is whether they are sound guidelines. After all, we are always talking of people who are young for their age, or old for it. Take birth, for a start. It is considered within the normal range for babies to be either 5 lbs or 10 lbs, and yet both are promptly given the same age if they arrive on the same day. Babies of less than 5 lbs are frequently born, and frequently survive; so too babies over 10 lbs. In other words, some of us arrive in this world four times heavier than others. Weight isn't everything, but it is one indication of maturity at that starting time of life, and it is fair to generalise that a heavier baby ... is probably a maturer baby. It may have spent more time in the uterus, and therefore is more mature for that reason, but society doesn't care about gestation time. It puts down the birth-date, and that is that.

Let's now leap ahead to puberty. We can all remember at school when some of our equals in age suddenly leaped ahead in the sexual changes that transformed them from children into adults. They shot up in height. Their voices – if they were boys – cracked and then boomed. And as for their genitalia, well, they were very different from those in the shower room belonging to colleagues still emphatically children. We were all of an age, but you wouldn't have thought so by looking at us. According to the books, penis development associated with puberty starts on average at 13 and proceeds for about two years. But, entirely normally, it can start at 11 or at 14½. The completion of this development can, again normally, occur at 13½ or at 17. So some boys will have finished this particular aspect of their development before others have even begun. And yet society goes on looking at their calendar age and not at their development. To have completed the pubertal changes doesn't necessarily make you better suited, for example, to ride a motorbike. But my point is that we are not born equal, and are certainly not equal physically during the time of adolescence when so many laws related strictly to age come into their own. I know that some of my schoolfellows would have been entirely competent with motorbikes at the age of 12 (and were so round the back of the yard) while others wouldn't have reached that degree of prowess until 18 or so. But the State lumps them all into the same category. It says you can ride a motorbike 5,844 days after your birth-date, and not a single day earlier whoever you are. You just have to wait for the earth to make 16 complete revolutions round the sun, to travel 4,675 million miles in orbit before you can travel your first inch on a motorbike.

At that same magic moment, and not a day before, you can also buy Premium Bonds, sell scrap metal, join a trade union (but you can't yet become a union executive), you can leave school (on the last day of the Easter term, for example, if you were 16 in the preceding September to January), you can choose your own doctor, you can have sexual intercourse if you are heterosexual or a lesbian (but male homosexuals can't do so until they are 21), you can work full-time but you can't, for example, start training to become an engine-driver for another ten months, you can leave home (with your parent's consent), you can marry (with your parent's consent), you can enter or live in a brothel (without your parent's consent), you can buy fireworks (provided you also look 16 to the person selling them), you can apply for social security benefit but you now have to pay for your dentures and your glasses (unless you are at school or college when the glasses still come free but not the teeth) and you can drive certain tractors, and an invalid carriage, and a motorbike.

If you had been one day younger, even if you had been shaving for years, and lusting for girls, and longing to leave home or sell scrap metal, you would not have been able to do any of those things. But, once you are 16, however immature in your general development, you would suddenly be able – in theory – to do all those things.

Now to a further stage in life. As everyone knows, one particular man or woman of 65 bears little relation, either physically or mentally, to some other man or woman of 65. 'Look at her,' we say. 'She's still doing all her decorating, and is good for another 30 years.' Which she probably is. 'Look at him,' we say. 'He may be the same age, but he can hardly get out of bed. He'll probably be dead in a year.' And he probably is. So one dies, of old age in effect, 30 years before the other. But the State doesn't see things that way. It says that men retire at 65, women at 60, and there's an end to the matter. It knows that a third of British businessmen die before reaching retiring age, and it knows that it's very exceptional for a woman to do so; but the ages are fixed. To be a male aged 64 and 11 months is to get none of the pension perks. The Earth has to stay in orbit just another 30 days, and then they come. It is, as I said at the beginning, a bureaucratic convenience of the highest order. It is also, in my opinion, extraordinarily unfair and for two reasons. The first relates to our development, and the second to what could be called ageism.

On development the happy idea of choosing a particular age before we can do anything can mean that that age on average is a good one for us to start doing that particular activity. At 17 we are allowed to drive a car, a far easier thing to do well, I think, than to ride a motorbike well, which we can do one year earlier, but that is by-the-by. On average, therefore, the State has decreed that we are fit to start driving at 17. This also means, averages being what they are, that about half of us are fit to drive before that time and the other half are still not fit to drive a car. So, half have been held back and half are given permission before they are ready. In other words, on this compromise, it's unsatisfactory for absolutely everyone.

Anyhow, at 18 we can leave home, marry, vote, get a passport, buy on hire purchase, own a house, become an executor, make a will (although we can join the Army beforehand where they let us make wills earlier), change our name, sue someone, be sued, go abroad for 'the purposes of singing, playing or performing or being part of an exhibition without a licence', buy drinks in a pub (although we've been allowed to play dominoes and cribbage there for the past four years), sit on a jury, buy and sell goods, and get a mortgage. However, we can't sell alcohol, or be a candidate for a by-election, or drive a heavy goods vehicle until we're 21; we can't drive a train until we're 25, but we can fly a plane when we're 17.

Every now and then there are small chinks in all this inflexibility. For instance, you can go to an X film not only when you're 18 but when you're too young, in the manager's view, to make anything of the movie, such as a babe in arms. And you can't buy fireworks until you're 16 or look, in the opinion of the shopkeeper, as if you are 16. And the same sort of thing goes for drink-buying; you can be refused if, in the publican's view, you aren't 18. What there isn't is the same sort of law the other way round, namely that the manager is allowed to sell you drinks if you look mature enough to handle the alcohol, or the X film, or the tobacco, or the fireworks. In short, maturity doesn't really come into it. The crucial thing is your age, the number of birthdays you have had, and not the degree of development you have undergone in all that time.

Now to ageism, if there is such a word as yet. If not, in these more liberal days when racism and sexism have had such a hearing, there certainly ought to be. In general we can no longer discriminate against people because of their race or because of their sex, but we can because of their age. And we do. On one page of *The Times* advertising vacancies there were 31 discriminatory references to age. 'Must be 21.' 'Aged 19 to 22.' 'Executive secretary 28 to 35.' 'P/A secretary 23 plus.' 'Someone special 26 to 36.' 'Secretary 20s.' 'Personnel Services Assistant 25 to 30.'

And suddenly there was one, one on the whole page, which said, 'Age completely immaterial' – for a telephonist. Judging by that one page, mainly of secretarial type jobs, it must be very difficult getting employment if you are under 20 or over 35.

As I see it, we may prefer to have someone of this or that race, or this or that sex, but we are not allowed to discriminate solely on these grounds. So, why are we allowed to discriminate over age? Shouldn't ability be the only thing we are entitled to look for? Either the person can do the job better than the other applicant, or the person cannot. It's as easy as that, or should be. Similarly, at the other end of the scale, we all know of men who should have been retired long before they were 65. And of others who are still fine at that age. Age discrimination has nothing to do with getting the unemployment figures down, but has a lot to do with not wanting to pay someone a pension, with secretaries being prettier when they're younger, and less able to run an office when they're too young, and more likely to want to stay if they're 35 or so. There are always reasons for discrimination, whether the rest of us think they're valid or not, but I hope we become less ageist in the future, just as we have become less racist and less sexist in the very recent past.

A final thought – on age. In 1952 Christopher Craig and Derek Bentley together shot a policeman. Craig, aged 16, pulled the trigger. Bentley, aged 19, allegedly encouraged him to do so. Craig was too young in years to be hung. Bentley, although he still couldn't vote at the time, or marry without parental consent, was old enough to be hanged. He had had sufficient birthdays. So they hanged him.

Women

In these days, when we all rush around saying how equal everybody is, it's very easy to forget all our inequalities. And when boys and girls even dress alike, so that jeans and long hair at a hundred paces look extraordinarily uniform, we seem to be trying even to diminish the outstanding fact that we have two, widely different sexes. Of course, life would be inexpressibly dull if we were all alike, and unthinkably different if we were all of one sex, but I want to take a look at one sex difference, always very noticeable in the past, that may be diminishing. Or ought to be diminishing, or is even more fascinating if it's not diminishing. I am referring to the different kinds of disease that men and women get.

By this I don't mean the masculine and feminine complaints that can't be suffered by the other half. More intriguing, to my mind, are the various illnesses and reasons for death that ought to be experienced equally, such as heart disease, peptic ulcers, cancer in general, or influenza - all of which, and many more, kill men much more than women. The really intriguing point, I think, is whether this situation is changing. If women are leading lives more like men these days, going out to jobs and worrying about their jobs, oughtn't they to be getting the ulcers that men used to get - and still do?

But, before getting on to this point, it's as well to remind ourselves that males and females are very different kinds of human being. Of course, there are the basic differences, the primary sexual characters, but hard upon their heels are the secondary sexual characters, such as breasts - for women, and facial hair - for men. Women and men do not have the same quantities of hormone circulating in their bloodstreams and these, apart from giving rise to quite different secondary sexual characters, must also have effects that we don't know about yet. Perhaps a stomach is affected in some way by testosterone, perhaps not, but it certainly could be.

Anyway, there's also a third set of differences between the sexes, measurable differences that don't seem to have much to do with sex. Women, for example, are – among Europeans – about 6 inches shorter than men. Their brains are, on average, about 10 per cent smaller. Their metabolism is less demanding; weight for weight they need less food. They've got about 10 per cent fewer red blood cells in every pint of their blood. And, one way or another, this all adds up to less strength, less speed, less endurance. To generalise for athletics, women at sea-level are about as good as men at 7,000 ft altitude. But, in another sense, men are undeniably the weaker sex. More miscarriages are of boys. More stillbirths. And more deaths in childhood. At the far end, as we all know, men die earlier than women, by half a dozen years or so.

In other words, it isn't just that men have a penis and women a vagina. There are differences all along the line, and seemingly wherever you care to look. So, the fact that this or that disease strikes more vehemently at this sex rather than the other becomes less surprising. There are two kinds of body, and each is likely to be less or more susceptible to this or that disease. The inequality is blatant if you look at the sex-ratios for the common causes of death, and how men or women succumb to them.

Well, the figures for the 15 most common causes of death in the United States are very striking. In all but one of them men are the greater victims. So, to rattle off the 14 out of the 15 where men succumb more than women, the afflictions are heart disease, cancer, strokes, accidents, flu and pneumonia, baby diseases, arteriosclerosis, bronchitis and its allies, cirrhosis, congenital malformations, murder, kidney disease, peptic ulcer and suicide. In all of them American men do worse than American women. At first glance, the list includes just about every disease we can think of; but, as women do die of something, they just make a different list. The important point is that the kind of death is very different between the two sexes. The only one of the common 15 to kill women more frequently than men is diabetes mellitus, slightly to be expected as it has a relationship with the menopause.

Now to the changes, and whether women have, in recent

years, been getting not just more rights and wages, but a fairer share of the male diseases. The answer overall is: No. Of those 15, and again using American figures, the men have in general been suffering even more. Comparing the figures of 1950 with those of 1969 the men are dying relatively more from heart disease, more from cancer, more from strokes, more from accidents, more from flu and pneumonia, much more from bronchitis, slightly more from cirrhosis and more from kidney disease. The female figures show rises relative to men only for suicide, murder, arteriosclerosis, and peptic ulcer but, despite these relative rises, the four diseases still kill off more men than women. As for diabetes mellitus women still die from it more than men, but now by a smaller margin.

What's harder to detect from the figures is whether men are getting fewer of the job-aggravated diseases because their wives are working more. In a fair world – which I admit is a quaint notion – if women are shouldering more of the load, and worrying more about their jobs, men ought to be shouldering less of the load and worrying less about their jobs. If heart disease and the like are partly brought about by job-worry and ambition, not only should women be getting these diseases more but men should be getting them less. We shall see. At present these are early days, and women haven't been in the competitive arena long enough for the mortality figures to show up these final effects of all the recent changes in our joint way of life.

The business of getting lung cancer by smoking cigarettes is hardly an equality issue; women have been entitled to buy cigarettes and smoke them ever since the things began. But women didn't actually smoke much relative to men until fairly recently, and perhaps increased equality did help them to take up the habit. But now they have done so with a vengeance. In my experience, women smoke more than men, but the facts still show that men are maintaining their lead, although by a narrower margin than ever before. What did seem to be unfair for quite a while was that women appeared almost immune from lung-cancer whereas men were certainly not. But those days have gone now. Women smokers are getting the disease and catching up the men. As with other

afflictions linked with styles of life, it just takes time
before a changing habit shows up as changing figures in
the mortality tables.

Apart from dying differently, there are other persistent
quirks associated with women. Despite living longer, and
therefore being more of a biological success, women make
use of doctors much more than men, they have more
operations, they make more visits to hospitals, and more
prescriptions are made out on their account. As they do
live longer all of this could provide a sound argument for
making use of doctors and hospitals; the more you visit
them, it seems, the longer you live. But perhaps it's not
that simple, and women visit doctors more because it's
easier for them to do so, or society is more tolerant of them
doing so, or doctors encourage them to be more dependent
upon the medical services. Take your pick.

It's also odd that boys (certainly in America and
probably here as well) both visit doctors and stay in
hospitals more than girls. Can this be because boys *are* the
weaker sex and therefore have more need of treatment? Or
because mothers - dread thought these days - care more
for their boy children? Or because boys take less care of
themselves, both in getting into accidents and not
worrying that they wear wet clothes? Who knows? That's
the fun of human studies. Experiments are so difficult,
and therefore hypotheses can flourish without much fear
of contradiction.

Even if women smoke as much as men, and in some
quarters seem to drink as much as men, and often get fat
as much as men - all of which must affect the kinds of
disease they get - I wonder to what extent they will bother
to invade traditionally masculine precincts now open to
them. In other words, will they render themselves more
liable to be affected by the job-linked diseases that now
plague men? Heaven alone knows, but there are all sorts of
indicators which seem to show that women do not favour
certain styles of life, however accessible. I am not about to
embark on listing the lack of women chess players,
mathematicians, composers and so on, but I do find it
strange that there are so few women MPs, and FRSs, and
captains of industry. Male prejudice can't account for

everything. Even at the trivial level I've wondered why so few women become glider pilots, or even - in my own sport - balloon pilots. It's barely 10 per cent in either activity.

Well, we can all wonder like anything, and wonder just how many females will leap at the chance, now proposed by the Pentagon, to become combat troops and fly combat aircraft, but my suspicion is that the two sexes are a lot more different than we give them credit for in these days of unisex. I just do not believe that attributes like ambition, and frustration, and the ability to be unhappy, and a yearning for recognition, and a love of power, are evenly divided between the sexes. Consequently, I don't believe that the stress-linked diseases which relate to such characteristics will ever be evenly suffered by the two kinds of people. But we shall see.

Much of the information for this talk came from an excellent paper in the *New England Journal of Medicine* by Charles E. Lewis and Mary Ann Lewis, both from a Department of Medicine in Los Angeles. It is, therefore, fair to give them the last word. 'If,' they write, 'we are striving for a non-sexist society, with equal opportunity for all, it would be better to seek increased opportunities for women in occupation, business and commercial affairs, and a reduction in the morbidity and mortality of men. Perhaps, so the Lewises conclude, 'this proposition evades the fundamental question: What is the better measure of equality; for women to die like men, or for men to live (a little bit) like women?' Well, what's it to be, if those are the alternatives? For women to have a richer, shorter life? Or for men to have less power and live a little longer? Probably it'll be a bit of both, but I'm sure we'll never be equal.

Athletics

The idea came to me when I was watching a bunch of Xavante Indians in Brazil doing a kind of relay race. It was reinforced when I went walking with a Masai in eastern Africa. And it was engrained for ever when I heard that the nearby Watusi, a sizeable bunch of people whose males average 6 ft 5 in, actually like high-jumping. The idea was that I should combine all these people, and a variety of others scattered around the globe, into a special Olympic team, a kind of ethnic entry which would sweep the board. Following precedent in the world of cricket, and giving happy reign to my ego, I thought of calling them Mr Smith's Eleven.

But, before getting on to the particular merits of my team, there are certain fundamental reasons behind the idea. The first is that I personally don't like the nationalism in such events as the Olympic Games. I don't like the competitors, all dressed alike for each nation, marching behind their national flags. And I don't see why there have to be all those national anthems, and national scoreboards. May the best man win, of course, and may he win fairly, but there is nothing fair about the sizes of all the competing nations. How on earth can Luxembourg vie with the Soviet Union? In the old Olympics, in Greece, did Sparta compete against Thrace or was it man against man, irrespective of his sphere of government? Certainly, that's how I'd like to see the Olympic athletes enter the stage, a great morass of people from the planet, all come together to compete against each other. And if there is to be a scoreboard, it's for individuals and not for nationalities.

The second fundamental reason for my team is that they're the sort of people who are never going to get into any kind of national team. Currently, they're still the people they used to be, the isolated groups who have maintained their own way, genetically and culturally. In time, probably, their ethnic individuality will become submerged in the great welter of mankind. Their culture, which may have concentrated upon a particular brand of athletics, will almost certainly go for they will just become citizens of the nation that has grown up around them. No longer will they be the unique reservoir of talent that I wish to draw on to make up my very special team. Right now, owing to their remote circumstances, and to the fact that they are not yet conventional members of the modern world, they do not enter the arena. Just as the first modern Olympics – in 1896 – witnessed only 285 athletes selected from 50,000 or so thought to be in training at that time throughout the world, so do today's big events only select men and women from a fraction of the global population. Ask any Indian in Brazil what he thinks of the Olympics, and he will not know what they are.

Hence the background to my team. It will be an international assortment, a gathering from all over, a collection of people who, as things stand at present, are not collected by the countries in which they live. More important, because the real aim of every athlete is not the taking part but the winning, my team – as I have said – would sweep the board, wipe the floor, bring home the bacon. In a word, they'd win.

So, to explain this firm conviction, let's go back to the Xavante of Mato Grosso state in central Brazil, and to the first time I ever saw them run. Until that moment I had seen them fishing, and smoking, and generally lounging about, which three activities leave little time for much else; but I had seen that they were immensely strong. They have chests like barrels, bodies to match and even their feet look powerful. Well, came the day when I first saw them run. They called it the Buriti race, after a species of palm tree. Others might call it a relay race because the aim was not to get a man past the winning post but the baton that was carried. Unlike the standard baton, a relatively lightweight thing, this one tipped the scales at around 200 lbs. It was a section of Buriti trunk – hence the name of the game – being about two feet long and one foot thick. A normal baton is carried lightly in the hand, but this one was shouldered like a bag of coal. The normal relay-runner waits at some appointed place until the minute burden is handed to him, but the Xavante all ran round the track shouting encouragement at their fellow with the hunk of palm tree. All were ready to take the load from him when he became a little puffed but everybody cheered and cheered until the best team set its colossal baton over the winning line.

Without doubt the Xavante would be among those I would select. I'm not certain what kind of race I would enter them for, as I assume the current relay rules will not be amended to make the batons several hundred times heavier. However, I do feel certain that those barrel chests, and that extraordinary strength, would come up trumps in some event. Perhaps the wrestling. Or the putting of the shot. Or even medium sprints like the 400 metres. Or just in intimidating the opposition as the Xavantes intimidated the Brazilian explorers for a couple of centuries.

I would also enter the Masai of eastern Africa for every walking race. They are supreme walkers, with bodies like bean poles. Not only do they stride across the east African savannah much as we walk across some city park, but their principal recreation is dancing up and down on the spot much as we never do. Their legs don't seem to bend when they touch the ground but merely spring again as if they're indiarubber. Which they may well be, for the Masai don't seem to consume food in the manner that we do. I remember once turning up to spend the night at a Masai encampment. Other arrangements had gone amiss, and I and two companions arrived hungrily and very tired. We explained that we had not eaten since breakfast and, in time, they brought us each a mug of milk. What nectar it was, and we all asked for another. Expressing amazement at such indulgence they did bring another, and that was that. Nothing would induce them that human beings could actually want or need more nourishment.

But whether it's their diet, or their shape, or their style of life, they do make excellent walkers. Some Americans once visited Masailand with a most fiendish treadmill. Its flat moving platform started off horizontally at some four miles an hour. At the end of every minute it increased its angle from the horizontal by one degree and maintained that relentless pace. At the end of 10 minutes the walkers on its platform were therefore striding up a slope of 10 degrees at the same four miles an hour. Well, the American athletes who had been training on this very machine for six months fell off with exhaustion when the angle slope had reached 25 degrees or so. The Masai, who had never seen the thing before, and who didn't really get the point of walking without getting anywhere, nevertheless all beat the top American. More amazing still, the Masai pulse rates had gone up during the exercise but not their respiration.

So, along with the Xavante, I would certainly welcome the Masai to my team. So too the Watusi. These people live west of Masailand and are taller still. The average male height is 6 ft 5 in, but many of them come close to 7 ft. More important still, from my Olympic point of view, they actually like high-jumping. It is their national pastime and, so I understand, their cross-bar is a length of rope tied between two trees. It would seem that the second national pastime must be breaking their legs, but I imagine they have learned how to land successfully even after failing to clear the unyielding length of rope.

The reason I would welcome the Watusi is partly because of that phenomenal average height. It is all very well in athletics possessing the drive and determination to win, but you must have the right kind of body as well. To be a top-class high-jumper you have to be tall. Similarly, to be a top-rank shot-putter, or discus-thrower, you really have to be over 6 ft. To be that tall means, probably, that you have long arms, and a longer arm is better mechanically in throwing such things. In the running events it is also best to be the right size and shape. In general, the longer the race the shorter the man who, on average, wins it. Shorter men are lighter and it plainly pays not to have to carry too much body along the track. At one Olympic Games it was found that the very heaviest marathon runner taking part was 10 lbs lighter than the very lightest 400 metre runner. It does pay to have the right kind of body for the gruelling task ahead. So, I would undoubtedly choose the Watusi to be my high-jumpers. Not only are their bodies tall but they actually like the sport.

Who else? Well, I would certainly use the Dinkas for
something. These people, who live around the White Nile, are
also tall but their legs are phenomenally long. I am 6 ft 3 in
and many Dinkas are my height, but on standing next to
them I was amazed to observe that their navels were six
inches higher than mine. In other words, their chest, neck
and head were relatively squat, and an extraordinary
amount of their height was taken up by leg. Well, they
don't high-jump, as a people, and they don't go off on
marathon walks, like the Masai, but I would certainly
have them in my team. Those legs would make them win
at something, say hurdling. And talking of legs I would
also recruit some porters from Kathmandu. When walking
in the Himalayas it is the custom to have all your gear,
tents, food and bedding, carried in 70-lb loads by men
about half your size. Worse still, while you are labouring
under the weight of one notebook and a ballpoint pen, they
overtake you in order that camp shall be ready before you
arrive. And worst of all you notice, as they pass by, that
they don't have muscles in their legs. They are just bones
with an occasional sinew linking the joints. Once again, I
do not know what they would win, but I would certainly
have them in my team.

As long-distance runners I would have to include the
Tara humara Indians who live in northern Mexico. Bruce
Tulloh, the British athlete, once travelled to their home to
discover their potentialities. He found an individual
named Ramón who had once won a race of 161 miles in two
days and a night. Tulloh himself took part in an event
where the laps were each 15 miles long. And he learned
that 12-year-old boys had recently competed against each
other in an 8-hour race. In Europe no women race over
more than 3 miles of cross-country, but Tulloh watched the
Tara humara women set off for 60 miles. So, welcome
aboard to these people from Mexico who, incidentally, do
all their running at around 7,000 feet.

What a team it would be – Xavantes, Masai, Watusi,
Nepalis, Dinkas, Tara humara, and anyone else I came
across who was not only exceptionally qualified but who
would never become involved in the normal, national,
selection process. How they would sweep the board, and

stand tall or short or very solidly upon the winner's rostrum. As for their anthem there would be silence, giving us all time to think how the small, individual groups of mankind have been and are being absorbed into the great mass of people of the world.

But, alas, it's all a dream. It wouldn't work. I know the Xavantes would prefer to fish. I'm sure the Masai would prefer to stride among the big game of the land they used to own. Such people have survived because they are not part of the common herd, and have no wish to be. They would listen to me politely as I tried to recruit their interest, and then politely ignore my strange request. So, the Olympics will continue with national flags, and national anthems, and national scoreboards. And my international team will fish, and walk, and jump, just as they have always done, until the world swallows them up for good.

Talking to Strangers

The other day I was sitting in the sun in Italy. A nearby church had looked warm and comfortable. So I sat down on its steps, closed my eyes, and basked. Not long afterwards a voice said:

'Hello. My name is Donatella. I am 4½ years old. What is your name?'

For the next couple of minutes I was fairly hectically involved in a question and answer session about brothers, sisters, aunts, where she got her new socks from, how a brother had a new pair of shoes but she didn't, and how old I was. Eventually, and abruptly, as if the moment had come for some urgent appointment elsewhere, she went, glancing neither left nor right but wholly at her socks. I had been enchanted by the chat and, as the sun then gave up, I too left the scene.

But her company had been fun, and how nice it was that a young girl could approach a stranger. In Britain we seem to have very strong views that children should not approach strangers. We are extremely aware that such close encounters of this kind can lead to tragedy. In fact, we have only to read in the papers that some child is missing from home for us to start assuming that an unclothed and mangled body will be found, either sooner or later, on a nearby common, or on a not-so-nearby common the child must have reached by car. As a nation we are intensely aware that death can lurk in the presence of strangers in black cars proffering bags of sweets. I have even had it argued to me by a Brazilian that she would not come to England for fear that her children would be assaulted in this fashion. It would seem that we have achieved renown in this regard, if only because our newspapers mirror our own interest by giving such prominence to the cases that do happen. My query is whether such cases *are* frequent and whether we are not guilty of over-reaction.

So, let's have a look at some facts. More important, let's try and see them in proportion to other potential mishaps. A fairly frightening fact to start off with is that a quarter of all the victims of either murder or manslaughter committed in this country are under 16 at the time of their death. These days, following a revision of the definition of homicide, there are six different kinds of murder and manslaughter, such as normal murder, insane murder, murder related to suicide, and so on, and some of these categories fare even worse than that general proportion of a quarter. For instance, with common-law manslaughter there were 61 victims in a recent four-year period and 51 of these were less than five years old. In that same four-year period, a total of 400 children, all of them under 16, were victims of either murder or manslaughter. It would seem, therefore, that that Brazilian woman was quite right; children in Britain are often done to death.

But let's read on. In the booklet from which I'm quoting (*Homicide in England and Wales 1967–71*) there's a sentence which suddenly shifts one's thinking about all that death: 'The child victims were mainly sons and daughters of the suspects'. Apparently in the normal murder category 57 per cent were killed by their parents; in common-law manslaughter the proportion was 86 per cent and in abnormal murder and section two manslaughter the proportion was 90 per cent, that's nine out of every 10 children done to death by their parents. Apart from the parents, who did a total of 81 per cent of the child killings over that four-year period, most of the other killers were either relatives or acquaintances of their victims. So, of the total of 379 victims of the cleared-up cases, 307 were killed by their parents, 7 by other relatives, 40 by acquaintances (such as the mother's new lover) and 25 by strangers. That's 25 out of a total of 379, or 6.6 per cent. Therefore, from a more realistic point of view, children should be warned first about their parents and only latterly about strangers. For children under one they should be most chary of their natural mothers as these killed 60 per cent of those who died, with foster parents killing a large proportion of the remainder.

However, although we destroy hundreds of children

each year on the roads, and murder or manslaughter
about 100 more each year as well, our major interest –
judging from the space given by the newspapers – is in
those cases where children are killed following a sexual
assault. It is these kinds of death the Brazilian lady was
speaking about, and it is these deaths that enter our
thoughts as soon as we read that some child is missing on
her, or his, way home from school. Well, in the same four-
year period, there were 20 deaths of children under 16
where the motive was considered to be sexual. That's less
than seven per cent of the total. Of course, it's bad that any
child should die in this way, just as it's bad that any child
should be killed in any manner, but it is good I believe for
the rest of us to know the facts, to know the proportions
that are involved, the scale of the problem. Of the 20 sexual
deaths – or five a year – it can be presumed that quite a few
of them, if not the majority, were caused by friends,
relatives or parents of the children concerned. The stranger
in the black car proffering sweets is our conventional idea
of the child-killer, but he certainly doesn't loom large in the
cold-blooded homicide and criminal statistics published
by Her Majesty's Stationery Office.

In other words, of the five sexual child deaths a year, we
can't do much about those that were committed by
parents, relatives or friends. Of course, the children will
get into the cars of such people, or walk across the common
with them, or accept sweets, although it may prove fatal
for them to do so. As for the strangers, those who kill
perhaps two, perhaps three children a year for deformed
sexual reasons of their own, I suspect they can produce a
fairly convincing story to the child because they may well
have been observing that particular child. They may say
that Auntie Flo, who usually comes to the bus-stop, has
her Uncle George to stay again, that her foot – which was
bad at breakfast – has got worse, and here's your favourite
ice-cream which you always get on Fridays. It must be
very difficult for a child not to be disarmed by that kind of
corroborative talk, with all its up-to-date information.
Adult males, however deformed their lusts, are quite likely
to be more cunning than the children.

As a society, we not only have – in my opinion – a very

exaggerated view of the likelihood of a sex-inspired murder of our children, but the same point is hammered home to us, for instance on TV. Some of those public service announcements, which tell us to save water or switch off electricity, also instruct us to tell our children about strangers. Here's a quote from one of them: 'It's impossible to think that anyone would want to harm our children, but we've only got to read the papers to know that these things do happen. When they're young, I know we do our best never to let them out of our sight. But when they're older – I know we can't wrap our children in cotton wool – but as parents we must warn them and keep on warning them. They mustn't go for a ride in a strange car. They mustn't talk to strangers or take sweets from them.'

What is quite unthinkable, of course, is that we should warn the children against their parents who do most of the killing. But we warn them against all strangers because, every once in a while, one particular stranger makes a lurid case by assaulting one particular child. Because of this we are apparently attempting to create a society where children are alarmed about all strangers and where strangers, such as old people longing for company, are alarmed in case their friendliness towards children is misconstrued. Yet old people can have a special rapport with children, being content with their kind of talk, having time on their hands, and loneliness, and a longing for past days which children can soften. I heard tell of an old man the other day who was 'warned off', as the saying goes, from giving sweets to children. Neighbours had complained and the neighbours got their way. But old people can kill themselves just out of loneliness. And they do, not in twos or threes but in their hundreds.

Naturally, no one is likely to advocate that children should go home with every stranger who asks them to, but perhaps we should be less besotted with the idea that strangers are suspect. And up to no good. Or murderers. Perhaps we should worry more about parents. After all, as we've seen, they do the bulk of the killing. I remember once seeing a very small child being hit again and again and again by a very angry woman. A man moved to protest,

but the woman told him to clear off as she was the child's
mother.

'Oh, that's all right then,' said the man.

And so said the rest of us who were in the park that day.
But if someone, some stranger, had offered a bag of sweets
to that same child, what would we have said? Would we
call a park attendant, and tell him of an errant, brutal
mother or of a man whose only observed attributes to date
were giving talk, comfort and some sweets?

In Italy, after my chat with Donatella, I saw a small boy,
crying and hopelessly lost.

'Papà, papa,' he sobbed.

I hesitated, wondering what to do. Then a man, not a
woman, also heard the boy and went straight to him.

'Have you lost your father?' he said.

The boy's face improved at once when confronted with
such a magical divining of his problem, and the two of
them chatted for a while about the possible location of the
missing father. Then, hand in hand, they left the scene. I
liked that. I've no idea what the Italian figures are for
sexual assault on children. I don't really care. I just feel
that they've got a better relationship between children
and strangers. And I'm sure that can't be bad.

Life and Limb

In the chemistry class they used to tell us that the human body was worth about five bob. Melt it down, split it into its various salts and compounds, and you don't get much for your labour. But in the law courts they think rather differently. There they have very firm ideas, not so much about the worth of the whole body, but about those bits of it that get lopped off or are otherwise rendered useless in, say, an accident. No one goes around saying how much two hands are worth if properly attached to two good arms, but they get very excited if one of those hands is severed, or just one finger, or one finger joint. You can get money if you lose one joint. You can get money if you lose anything, from the smallest part of you right up to your reason. You don't get much, in fact very little, if you lose your life, but there is a kind of sliding scale for virtually everything else.

These days the sums being paid out as damages for injury are getting bigger and bigger. Admittedly, there's inflation, but they're getting bigger in real terms. Partly I suppose because of a greater social conscience on behalf of those who are innocent victims of someone else's negligence. Partly because one successful case encourages others to succeed. And partly because they - the big companies and the big insurance firms - have so much money that we want more of it. Sueing for damages, particularly in America, is increasingly the thing to do. At all events, your little finger has never been worth so much. Or rather it's worth absolutely zero until you happen to lose it.

So, how much is it worth, not when it's attached but when some accident relieves you of its company? Let's look at recent court cases, in which people have lost all manner of bits and pieces and have been rewarded with fat cheques - or thin ones. But, first, don't forget that there's got to be someone to sue if you want to get any money. It's no good dropping an axe on your finger, and then hoping to get money from the axe company. Or from your wife who told you she'd just smashed the car, a fact which made you drop the axe in the first place. There has to be someone for you to be versus, someone who can be made to pay.

Anyway, to some cases to show how much your body is worth – when you lose a bit of it. Let's start with the finger. In a case last year a 62-year-old right-handed man lost the ring finger of his right hand in a car accident. This meant he couldn't play the piano or church organ any more and he got £2,750. Another man, aged 39, got his right middle finger trapped and lost two-thirds of an inch. He got £750. Averaging out those two cases, fingers are, therefore, worth about £900 an inch – when you lose them. Now to all the fingers. A married, childless, right-handed woman aged 42 lost all hers from the right hand and part of her thumb in a machine, and got £25,000. That's rather more than £900 an inch, but in view of losing them all from one hand it seems fair enough. Not actually losing a hand, but just damaging it, of course gets rather less. A 43-year-old man had a five-ton hammer fall on his right hand. Amazingly nothing was broken but, less amazingly, his wrist and fingers stayed stiff and swollen making it hard for him to lift things, work levers, climb ladders. His compensation was just under £4,000.

What about a bit of a leg? Well, a 12-year-old boy fractured his right femur, and that leg ended up half an inch shorter than the other. That half-inch got him £1,400. A 40-year-old man suffered a compound fracture of all three of the main bones in his right leg. After a long time in hospital, and being out of work for quite a while, he ended up with that leg 2 inches too short and, as compensation, he received £6,500. So leg inches on these two cases alone, are worth about £3,000 each. As against £900 for each finger inch.

To lose a whole leg, as happened recently to a 30-year-old unmarried man, is of course more severe. A gate fell on him, his leg had to be amputated, and the accident also diminished his sexual function by 50 per cent because his back was injured. I'm not quite certain about the precision of that 50 per cent sexual loss, and how such things are measured, but it alone got him £11,000. His leg loss, which also halved his potential, got him £17,000 and he received another £1,500 because his chances of job-finding were now less good if he became unemployed. All in all, the figure for losing his leg was therefore £29,500. While on the subject of sex loss, a man might consider the loss of a finger inch to be fair at £900 but what price would he put on his testes? Well, the courts have to think of a figure, and did so for an unfortunate 20-year-old who was not only knocked down by a car but then run over by another. Injuries were considerable, as might be imagined, such as a fractured pelvis and gross lacerations, but the man was also castrated. To get any sexual function at all he had to receive sex hormones implanted beneath his skin every six months, but psychologically and physically he had been considerably damaged by the accident. As compensation the court assessed general damages at £20,000. That's slightly less than the loss of a hand. I wonder, if we could vote on such things, how the rest of us would rate the loss of fingers, hands, legs – and testes – vis-à-vis each other.

The brain is the most costly organ. For example, a 12-month-old boy, born with a range of defects, was injected with a wrong and damaging solution. He suffered the maximum brain damage consistent with the continuance of life, and was expected to drag on for some 20 years as 'a vegetable'. He received nothing, of course, because he had been born wrong, but £31,318 because he had had extra wrongness thrust upon him. Such a precise figure implies correctly that assessments of damages are not just round figures pulled out of a hat, but careful additions of all the factors involved. With that wrongly-injected boy, for instance, he got £15,000 for loss of amenities, a word usually bracketed with pain and suffering; £750 for loss of expectation of life; £3,033 for loss of future earnings (over a five-year period); £8,000 for special accommodation in his home; £2,100 for travel between home and hospital; £1,635 for extra nursing by babysitter and mother; and £800 special damages to cover the cost of the action and so forth – all told £31,318. People might debate whether it was worth £900 to lose an inch of finger. No one, I feel sure, would ever argue that it was worth having a vegetable of a child for a certain sum of money. The money is there, not to right a wrong for that can never be achieved, but to try and lessen the blow where money can serve a useful purpose.

However, the sums do vary. The British record for brain damage to date was to Dr Lim Poh Choo who, at the age of 41 and when undergoing minor surgery, was disastrously starved of oxygen owing to an error in the hospital. In the High Court she was awarded £243,000. That's over seven times as much as the 12-month-old boy got, but Dr Lim was a consultant psychiatrist who had, to put it crudely, lost much more by the error than a one-year-old mal-formed boy. Her future earnings alone, which were part of that enormous sum, were assessed at £84,000. The defendants will have to pay this sum if their current appeal is not found acceptable, and one inevitably wonders how much less they would have to pay if Dr Lim had not recovered at all from the operation, if the error had been so grave that she had died instead. There used to be a terrible colonial remark that, in the event of running over a native, it was better to reverse and run over him again because a dead person was much less trouble than someone merely wounded. That truth can, on occasion, still be valid. For example, however much fingers are worth less than hands, and hands less than arms, and arms less than brains, the customary award in this country for loss of expectation of life, for being killed before your time, is £750. If, in an accident, you can stay alive and suffer for a couple of hours, you – or rather your relatives – are likely to get more.

In many ways the assessment of damages is an impossible task. Just how do you put a sum on the joy of having a right arm, of having a family, a pretty face, or a functioning brain? Besides, a lot of people are born without right arms, or brains, or sexual organs. You can't sue bad luck, or a wrong set of genes handed down by your parents. Similarly, if you just get ill during life, and this leads to the loss of your arm or brain, you can't do much about that. You can't sue a disease. However you can, in our society, get something from the State. You can receive a mobility allowance if you can't get about well. And there's attendance allowance if someone has to visit you. And invalidity allowance. And industrial disablement benefit. What there isn't from the State – which is why people go to court – is the extra compensation figure, the apology made in cash terms for having done wrong.

Take the famous Thalidomide story. The compensation money eventually paid to the victims of this drug was far in excess of the money that would have been paid by the State to the children had a culprit not existed. Thalidomide did not invent a new kind of congenital abnormality. It merely caused more children to be born possessing the abnormality of micromelia, of very short limbs. Between straight compensation and a trust fund, the makers of Thalidomide have paid about £100,000 to each of the children so far considered eligible for payment. The parents of natural short-limbed children, conceived after the drug was withdrawn, must wish that they too could sue someone and get that kind of money. Without doubt it's good to have a successful action in the courts and to get compensated in addition to all the social security benefits.

It's best of all to get punitive damages as well because these can be colossal and it's fascinating to wonder just who is being punished. Very often the bill is just passed on to the tax-payer, or the rate-payer, or future customers, i.e. you and me. The record for punitive damages was the £66 million recently awarded to a boy who had been badly injured in a Ford Pinto car. The court didn't like the way that Ford had coolly calculated just how much it might have to pay out if it put the petrol tank in a cheaper but more dangerous position. So, Ford was punished and the boy got the money which, if invested at 10 per cent, will bring him £16,000 a day.

But, even with this sum, the boy, now an 18-year-old, says he wishes the accident had never happened. He'd prefer an unburnt body to all that cash. So, hang on to the body that you've got. It's not only irreplaceable. It's also invaluable.

English

At the time of the Battle of Hastings, there were one and a half million people who could speak English. As everyone knows, we lost the battle and suffered an infusion of the French language. But English survived, although contained within Britain. In the reign of Queen Elizabeth I a headmaster pointed out that the 'English tongue is of small reach, stretching no further than this island of ours, nay not there over all'. That reach was to change dramatically. Within a few years the first settlers arrived in Virginia, all speaking English. A few more years and shiploads of other English-speakers were landing all over the globe. Whether settling for good, or merely administering, they took their English with them and spread this one language enormously. It is now the most widely spoken language on Earth, being the prime tongue of some 400 million people but the second tongue of millions more. It is *the* international language, the most favoured *lingua franca* of them all, in commerce, aviation, diplomacy, science. Its success has been explosive.

I am not saying this as a piece of jingoistic bombast, but merely to introduce the fact that those who have English as their mother tongue are in a very special category. Not only will they find fellow English-speakers all over the place, but they will meet all manner of other people longing to improve their English. This, of course, has the result of making English-speakers a fairly idle lot, in that they can get by almost everywhere just by speaking more clearly and a bit slower; but the idleness can be hard work at times. 'Oh, Mister, I love your beautiful English too much. Can I speak with you for the next four hours as I am not too busy?'

My feeling is that we English-speakers have not yet grasped the full meaning of our unique status. We have not yet adjusted the way we learn languages, in schools and in later life, to the most singular state in which the English language now resides. Nor are we taking any steps to prepare ourselves for the future in which our tongue will be even more important. I think this is excusable only because the English explosion is so recent, and some date it as starting from the end of World War Two. Of course, there were English-speakers in great numbers before then, notably in the places that had been or were our colonies; but that was an invasion of English more than an explosion. The current explosive trend is for the locals to impose it upon themselves. It is *the* second language. Almost every capital city in Asia and Africa has an English language daily. It was the language of the Bandung conference in the 1950s when delegates from 29 nations representing 1½ billion people gathered to harangue - among other things - British imperialism. When the Dalai Lama escaped from the roof of the world he was met by India's prime minister. 'How are you?' said Nehru in English. 'Very nice,' said the Dalai Lama.

Whereas the rest of the world has decided in large measure that it would like to learn English, I am less certain - in fact not certain at all - whether this dramatic turn of events has had any effect over here, for instance in our schools. My feeling is that it should have done. We are now in a novel situation, quite different from, say, 100 or even 40 years ago. And yet we go on learning French, for example, as our Number One second language just as we have always done, ever since it took over from Latin as *the* language to learn. But why French today? It is losing its power in the world, just as English is gaining, but what language should we replace it with?

Currently, French lies twelfth in the language stakes, being spoken by less than a hundred million people. Mandarin Chinese is first, with about 700 million, but almost all of these people live in China. It is not widespread as is English, which comes second with 400 million. Third is Russian, with about 250 million, but - as with Chinese - very little of this language is spoken outside the mother country. The thing about English is that it's the language with which a German checks into a Peking Hotel, it's what Tito of Yugoslavia used to talk with Sadat of Egypt, and it's what China and Russia mainly make use of to beam their message to the world. The fourth most widely spoken language is Spanish, which is used over half the landmass of South America, most of central America and in Spain. Learning Spanish makes a lot of sense. Number 5 is Hindi. That makes less sense, as it's another restricted language, and a lot of them do well in English. Next, in roughly equal numbers, come German, Bengali, Arabic, Japanese and Portuguese. Well, German is not the language it used to be, when it was the key language of science, but it is still very useful outside Germany, notably in eastern Europe. Bengali is another restricted tongue, but not so Arabic which is the dominant language of 22 separate nations. Japanese is really only good for Japan, but Portuguese does open up the whole of Brazil, namely half South America, as well as Portugal.

Then, twelfth in line in this Babel pecking order, comes French, spoken by 2½ per cent of the world's people, but losing ground in former strongholds, such as the old Indo-China and the French bits of the Middle East, like the Lebanon and Syria. However, it is still entrenched in British schools. A total of 152,000 children took O-level French a couple of years back, whereas only 62,000 took the next four most popular languages – German, Italian, Spanish and Russian. Putting that another way round it means that 60 per cent of our children learn to speak with 100 million people, while 40 per cent learn to speak with 700 million people. France may be our nearest neighbour, and probably the first place we go to when we go abroad, but it is odd that we still favour French to such a large degree. Even with A-levels, when children are more aware of the subjects that will be of most use to them, French is still dominant, with 52 per cent of the language papers being taken in that tongue. German, Italian, Spanish and Russian supply most of the other 48 per cent. Of course, there is all that French culture but culture also exists in Germany, Italy, Spain and Russia, although I am less certain that a French person would be quite so willing to concede this point. I liked the comment by a Swiss journalist that 'if a German wants to enlarge his intellectual horizons he will take up another language. A Frenchman will read more French'.

So, what should we English do (and just think of saying that sentence in French)? What should we do, apart from learning French as the majority of us do to a level that merely induces pain in the people of France? It is so easy to believe that we are bad linguists. We meet those Scandinavians who say, with near perfection, that they one year have been English learning, and we wonder what we were like after learning one year French.

Well, there are some 4,000 languages in the world, give or take a thousand according to your definition of a dialect. Most of these we can dismiss because but a handful of people speak them. However, there are 160 which are spoken by more than a million people, such as the 40 million who speak Turkish, the 30 million Thais, the 30 million Gujuratis, and the 1 million in Estonia. At once a grave weakness appears. Such languages are fine if you happen to be in Turkey, Thailand, India or Estonia, but they are useless - except for very chance encounters - everywhere else.

The British schools are at least attempting to favour international languages, save that their top two - French and German - are almost certainly on the decrease, whereas Spanish, which is on the up-and-up, is relatively rare in our schools (2,000 A-levels as against 26,000 for French). As for Arabic, also on the increase and increasingly important for trade, that is never even included in official exam figures. My personal experience in travelling is that French, such as it is, has not been of much use, and I have spent more time making use of such German, Italian and Portuguese that I possess. However, what I have spent most time doing, and this brings me to my final point, is in using English as a *lingua franca*. By this I do not mean that I speak English and they try to understand me. I mean that I adapt my English to their level and then try to understand them. It's no good saying 'Let's grab a bite in this establishment before it gets too late'. You have to adapt and say 'We eat here now?' or even 'Eat, yes?' according to the other fellow's proficiency. Of course, it's much nicer and more fun trying to speak his language, but there are so many of them wanting to learn English that we usually have to relent and have it their way.

Which all makes me wonder whether we oughtn't to be taught how to speak English to foreigners, to understand the very basis of our language that is probably the only bit of it comprehensible to them. We could learn what kinds of words in English are most likely to be understood by them, such as the Latin words for all the Romance people. What is the equivalent for the Arabic people? And do the Japanese find it easier if we try to speak their way, by leaving out all the articles? So too the Serbo-Croats? In fact ought we to be taught 'Language' as a subject, rather than any specific tongue?

I think we should. We are unique and we should realise this fact. I think it's high time we gave up 'la plume de ma tante est dans le jardin' and thought instead how to give the same piece of riveting news to an Indonesian. Or a Turkoman. Or even an Eskimo but, of course, it has to be in English.

Notice-Boards

I think that, as a nation, we are quite polite. When addressing strangers we don't say 'Tell me the way to Trafalgar Square'. We preface our request with all sorts of apologies: 'Excuse me. Very sorry to trouble you. But I wonder if you can possibly direct me along the way to Trafalgar Square?' Even small boys, not oustandingly famous as a group for politeness at all times, are not rude at their first encounter with a stranger. If we stray into some area, either deliberately or intentionally, where we should not be, the uniformed official is quite likely to say 'Can I help you, Sir?' At the back of his mind is 'What the hell are you doing here?' but the words come out differently, even if there is that powerful pause before the 'Sir'.

I believe we are a polite nation. We are, admittedly, foul about other drivers, but generally less so when they *do* run into us. Foreigners often express amazement at the cool way in which, over our battered machines, we exchange names and addresses. We are not always the very pineapple of politeness, to borrow Sheridan's phrase; but, in my opinion, we don't do too badly.

Hence my surprise at notice-boards. It would seem, judging from their manner, that behind our polite exterior is an insolent, pig-headed, offensive fascist longing to get out. And he does get out whenever there's a notice to be written. 'Keep Out' is about as charitable a statement as this other half of us can ever devise. We never say it to anybody's face, for if we did we would get our own face pushed in, but we certainly say it as soon as we get hold of a paint-brush and a notice-board. 'Strictly Forbidden' comes off our brush without a moment's hesitation, as does 'Prohibited By Order' and all manner of other remarks about Trespassers and Violaters of Bye-Laws. We would never, under normal circumstances, address each other like that and I wonder why we do so the

moment we speak to a wider audience. Even the friendly
notices, those designed to help, are equally blunt. 'The
public are prohibited on health grounds from collecting for
human consumption winkles, or other shellfish, from this
part of the foreshore.' Or 'These cliffs are dangerous. It is
strictly forbidden to climb them.'

It's almost as if some special sort of vitriol comes with
the paint that finds its way onto notice-boards. Even when
they're not being merely abusive, the notice-writers can't
use ordinary, nice-sounding words. For instance, 'Please
don't leave fish here' becomes 'It is an offence against
the council bye-laws to deposit any fish, offal or other
offensive matter on the beach slipways or promenade.
Any person doing so will be prosecuted.' Well, that notice
is offensive matter in itself, and *its* perpetrators ought to
be prosecuted. By the way, I'm not inventing any of these
belligerences, but I'm sure you know that. Anyone who
can read must have met dozens of them. 'Danger: Football
and cricket not allowed.' 'Bait Digging Totally Prohibited.'
'No dumping By Order.' 'Anyone defacing or ignoring this
notice will be dealt with according to law.' 'Do not loiter.'
'Keep Out.' 'No Landing.' About the only thing they don't
say is 'Drop Dead', but perhaps that's somewhere. They
certainly get close to it. 'Do not touch anything. It may
explode.' 'Warning. High Power Radio Waves. There is
little risk in short exposures. Prolonged exposures may be
harmful.'

Incidentally, I'm told that a notice exists which only
says 'Do not throw Stones at this notice'. The story is
credible for all sorts of other idiot injunctions exist, but
for true students of the notice-board the alleged wording is
quite incorrect. This should read 'It is strictly prohibited to
hurtle any object at or near this official sign installed by
Order Clerk of the Works'.

My query is whether such notices are counter-productive.
Suppose someone came to your door and you said, as your
opening words, 'Get Out', I suspect, whatever his previous
intentions were, the visitor might suddenly be impelled to
get in. Or at least push his boot in. In other words, a
normal person, obeying one set of unwritten rules about
politeness and normal social behaviour, can abruptly be

upset if he encounters another who is playing a different game. And in that upsetting he can be transformed from a law-abiding citizen into another who breaks the law just for the hell of it. 'Danger. Bicycling Strictly Forbidden' is an open invitation to some to start bicycling. And other offensive prohibitions will have him digging bait. Or parking on the shingle. Or playing football. Or whatever is disallowed.

The Americans, who tend to be wiser in their management of people, have a phrase for the Don't-Do-This-Or-That kind of notice. They call it negative sign-boarding, and believe positive sign-boarding is more effective. Instead of 'Don't go along there' they say 'This way to the Very Best View'. Most people, they argue, are not wanting to break rules but just wish to see the sight, to picnic, park their car, buy ice-cream and pitch a tent. So, if there are better places to do these things, why not tell them so. I once read in a Californian Forest that if I wanted to see the Redwoods to perfection I had better stand right here. Sure enough, that spot was much frequented and even its earth was worn away, but this meant that other spots, possibly with flowers growing on them, were less frequented. So, it wasn't 'Keep off the Flowers'; that's negative. Instead, it was 'Stand here for the best view of what you came to see'. All of a sudden, Authority seems to be on your side. Authority is there to help, and not just stop you doing things.

Suppose there's an area where rare birds nest and where the public should not go. The British approach, subtle as a sledgehammer, is to put up a sign: 'Keep Off. Birds Nesting'. That kind of warning, so they say in America, would have every passing American going out of his or her way to visit the area in question. What *they* do is to warn visitors that 'There are often snakes in this Area'. They don't instruct people to go away, but just mention the snakes and leave it at that. If further deterrent is required they often drop a large rock in the nearby stream. The water spills over the land, forms a bog and surrounds a notice saying 'This area is sometimes wet. A drier route lies in that direction'. No offensive language. No incitement to break the law. No mention of any law. Just helpfulness about how not to get your feet wet.

Perhaps the sign that most sums up both the belligerence of the British notice-board and its kind of phraseology is 'Trespassers will be prosecuted'. In legal language, trespass in England and Wales is a tort. It is a civil wrong and not a criminal wrong. Therefore, a mere trespasser cannot be prosecuted, as a prosecution can only be brought if a crime is involved. A trespasser may be sued, but I can't remember ever seeing a sign with those words upon it. However, I've seen lots about trespassers being prosecuted, and I wonder if there's any law about putting up signs which contain malicious untruths.

To be prosecuted for trespass in England and Wales the act of trespass has to be accompanied by damage, such as breaking fences or treading down grown corn. Most trespassers do nothing of the kind, and walking across a grass field or through woodland is unlikely to be damaging. If the landowner, or the tenant of the land, does decide to prosecute because of damage, and if he wins the case, he will only be able to get the amount by which the value of the property was diminished. In other words, how much was that particular bit of fence worth at the time, and not how much will it cost to put the fence back again. The average trespasser is probably not intent on doing damage and, even if some does result from his trespassing, the amount he does by accident is unlikely to be great. Of course, if he has a dog that goes berserk among a herd of pregnant ewes, that is a different story. But mere walking, mere trespassing, is unlikely to do great harm, if it does any harm at all.

In Scotland things are different. Trespassers cannot be prosecuted even if they have caused unintentional damage, but criminal proceedings can be started against those who squat on your land, or camp on it, or set foot with intent to poach, or who invade certain kinds of land, such as that owned by railways and dockyards. The ordinary person who does damage during his or her trespass in Scotland can only be sued, and not prosecuted unless the damage was malicious. Trespassing is therefore even less of a crime in Scotland than in England and Wales but the important point, remembering all those notice-boards, is that mere trespassers cannot normally be prosecuted in any part of Britain. They can be asked to leave the land, and must be allowed peaceably to do so, but I personally have never seen a notice to that effect. Neither have I seen a notice which says that the trespasser may even sue for assault if he is ejected with more force than is reasonable in the circumstances.

However, perhaps that is asking too much. What I am asking is that the thousands of our fellow citizens who put up notices, presumably with the wish that their injunctions may be followed, should pause before dipping paint-brush into paint. They should wonder if politeness might not coerce their readers more effectively than a frontal assault. They should ask themselves how they would like to be addressed. They should wonder if subtlety has perhaps a part to play. And they should then dip their brush not in the kind of carbolic acid most notice-writers use but in some gentler, wiser, humbler solution.

As notice-boards already litter the land, why not throw, well, a critical glance or two in their direction? Don't forget that it is strictly forbidden not to take offence at every insulting piece of phraseology being disseminated for our enlightenment by order.

Steele's Road Decoded

It all began one day when I realised that my workroom in London faced directly towards the pyramids at Giza. Admittedly, and somewhat nearer at hand, it also faced towards a block of flats, a bit of the railway line running north from Euston, the Nat-West pile, and something they are still building south of the river. But it faced Cairo nonetheless. You can see the Crystal Palace, as they used to sing, if it wasn't for the houses in between. Well, I could see straight to the pyramids if it wasn't for the curvature of the Earth *and* the houses in between.

This exciting realisation, which does improve the view, came after I had been immersing myself in books which instruct us that ancient objects, like the pyramids, are not just pyramid-shaped ancient objects. They are time pieces, astronomical telescopes, mathematical statements, and even predictors of the future. The Great Pyramid of Giza, for example, seems to be all those things and more. Did you know that the angle of descent and ascent of its sloping passages is 26 degrees, 18 minutes, and 9.7 seconds? More to the point, did you also know that, at the time the pyramid was built, this was the Pole Star's exact elevation from that latitude? Perhaps you did, and perhaps that isn't so very extraordinary; but, if that selfsame angle is laid off from the pyramid's east-west axis, it marks the bearing of the summer sunrise. And, if the line is projected, it goes through all sorts of interesting geographical sites, such as the town of Bethlehem.

Perhaps it's the Bethlehem bit that most sticks in the gullet. It's just too neat, by far. And a bit self-centred from a Christian point of view. Shouldn't an Egyptian pyramid be more interested in Medina or Mecca, or even – as a kind of compromise – Jerusalem? After all, as the pyramid was built almost 3,000 years BC, just about every historical event was in its future, and the birth-dates of Buddha, Christ and Mahommet were all at least a couple of thousand years ahead of its construction. The alleged facts are difficult to absorb. I can swallow hook and line, but not the sinker.

So, one wet day with rain drops obscuring even the nearest block of flats, let alone the transmission tower at Crystal Palace, I wondered about my room and where it pointed to. Well, with a compass I took a bearing, allowed for magnetic deviation from true north, and started to draw a line on the map. Fond hopes of heading straight for, say, Stonehenge were dashed, of course, as the window faced south-east; but I had high hopes of something significant in that line of sight. These were steadily diminished as it progressed through Holborn, Bermondsey, Deptford, Bromley, and then out into the Kent country through Borough Green, Mereworth, Benover, Mockbeggar, Sissinghurst, Woolpack, Reading Street, and Denge. Nothing significant among that lot, I had to confess, and still less on the French side.

Anyhow, I progressed further, trying to take account of great circles on Mercator projections, and felt I was getting warmer when the line passed through Alessandria in northern Italy, and then very near Rome, and then straight as a die, with excitement mounting apace, through the other Alexandria and along the delta of the Nile to Cairo. Who'd have thought that the structure in which I live, put up by simple folk all those years ago, should have harboured such a secret? Instead of pointing towards Bethlehem, or any other famous spot in the history of mankind – Runnymede, Hastings, Bosworth Field, Scunthorpe – the line headed straight for Giza, to that incredible point of origin, the original wonder of the world.

This was heady stuff, so heady that I went off mine and started measuring up my place of residence, just as the pyramidologists have done with such care on their even older piles. I counted the windows. I assessed the number of bricks. I found the length, and the height, and the breadth. I began to see the house with new eyes, getting a deeper insight into the possible reasons why those simple labourers of circa 1870, or the speculative overseers in charge of them, had arranged things. Formerly, I had thought it just irritating that a certain line of bricks

seemed to hiccup along its well-laid path. Now I wondered,
pondering over the message that that line of bricks could
contain. Any idea that it was just bad workmanship, or an
error, was now unthinkable. Certainly, the more I probed
the more astonished I became at the secrets lodged within
9 Steele's Road.

For example, I wondered at the number of bricks.
Allowing for the windows, the odd extras above the
doorway, and so on, I realised that some 511 square yards
of brick were used in this single structure. What was so
significant about this figure? Why 511? Or why 4,599
square feet of brick? I puzzled and puzzled, and resorted to
a builder who knew a thing or two, certainly about those
ancient times. Always used 50 bricks to a square yard,
they did, he said. I rushed back to the calculator. Fifty
times 511 is exactly 25,550. A light shone, brighter than
any Pole Star shining down a darkened passageway.
What is 25,550 but 70 years expressed in days. And what is
70 years but the lifespan allotted, in theory and according
to ancient texts, to every one of us. In fact, if we allow for
leap years, 25,550 bricks is about 17 bricks short of 70
years, and I knew I had solved the riddle of those
awkward, irritating kinks that I, in my short-sighted
twentieth century manner, had assumed to be crass
workmanship. Of course, of course, what could be more apt
than a brick line kink to represent each and every leap
year in our allotted three score and ten.

So, back to the calculator. There are 84 panes of glass in
the house and 26 windows, a seemingly bizarre arrangement with no apparent sense between the number of panes
in each window and its size. But, flushed with success, and
steeped in the kind of reasoning that has extracted such
formidable secrets from the ancient pyramids, I multiplied
26 by 84. The answer 2,184. And what is 2,184 but, as near
as dammit, 2,195. And what is 2,195 but the distance in
miles from London to Cairo. Eureka.

I persevered. To me the coincidences were, well, not just
coincidental. I measured the horizontal perimeter. With 26
feet across the front and 45 feet down the sides that came
to 142. That seemed to mean nothing. So, I measured the
vertical perimeter. With the same 45 feet down the sides

and 42 feet from the ground to the soffits, that came to 174. Again, it didn't seem to mean much. But think of perimeters and what's the most important perimeter in our planetary existence? Surely it's the perimeter of the Earth, a figure of 24,000 miles give or take a mile or two. So, I multiplied my two perimeters together, the vertical one of 174 and the horizontal one of 142, and hey presto the answer came to 24,700. Not quite perfect but another coincidence. And what was going on down on the Thames Embankment when all those bricks were being laid? Well, that was the very year when Cleopatra's Needle was being erected, after a turbulent crossing from Alexandria, within sight of 9 Steele's Road, that is if it wasn't for the houses in between.

All right; so I have been suffering from a surfeit of books explaining that the ancients were wise ahead of their time, were maybe extra-terrestrial, were not what we thought they were. It's more than enough to blow anyone's mind. For example, and I quote, 'the basic unit of measurement apparently used by the Great Pyramid's designer turns out to be an exact ten-millionth of the Earth's mean polar radius'. But that's not all. 'The pyramid's designed base-square has a side measuring just 365.242 of these same units, a figure identical to the number of days in the solar tropical year.' There's more to come. 'From the slightly indented shape of the base of the core-masonry alternative measurements of 365.256 and 365.259 of these units can be derived, figures which turn out to be the length in days of the sidereal year and of the anomalistic year.' These other kinds of year are important, but the greater importance of them in this context is that the Pyramid apparently tells us that it knew of their existence.

To go on, and to the calendar of events apparently pinpointed by the Great Pyramid. According to some it foretold the birth of a central messianic figure in AD 2, the achievement of full enlightenment by a central messianic figure on 1 April AD 33, and the central event of a period of destruction in AD 70 (the year that Jerusalem was sacked). Moving further forward it also predicted an idealistic time of physical turbulence between 1767 and 1848, the period that witnessed revolutions in America,

France, Austria, Hungary, Germany and Italy. It even
predicted, so some say, the rise and decline of an anti-
messiah between 1933 and 1944. Right now, it's busy
predicting a continuing decline of civilised societies.

Well, it could be argued that I'm not the only dotty one
around. Or that we're all mad in not concentrating every
possible resource into elucidating how on earth a building
put up nearly 5,000 years ago, and weighing 30 times as
much as the Empire State Building, could be quite so wise
and informative and capable of such devastating prediction even to the extent of as good as naming Adolf Hitler.
The Pyramid is either the greatest piece of news the world
has known, or it's just a heap of stones put together in such
a way that stretched the technology of the time to its
utmost. It either knocks our chronological thinking
sideways or leaves us precisely where we were. What an
extraordinary society we are that we pay gentle attention
to such colossal and shattering concepts as telepathy,
extra sensory perception, ghosts, astrology, prediction of
the future, extra-terrestrial visitations, and then pursue
the main business of the day, such as getting angry that
the toast was burnt, or the train was late, or that
telephoning connects us with all manner of irrelevant
people. If a spaceman *had* visited, or some being *had* filled
the Pyramid with incredible data, these creatures would be
astonished at our near-total indifference.

So, perhaps they can acquire a grain of comfort should
they take a glance at Steele's Road. Indifferent no longer, I
must find out just where the sun of the winter solstice, now
fast approaching, hits the lavatory wall, and why the
drainpipes are at 19 degrees to the vertical for 79 feet in all.
79,19? Or something fearful in 1979?

Fire Precautions

A committee was set up not too long ago to hammer out a new set of fire safety regulations, and it was composed almost entirely of senior firemen. Fair enough. Who could possibly know more about fires than senior firemen? They proposed, among much else, a greater preponderance of fire doors, so much so that an allegation was made, most unkindly, that the committee must have been composed of swing-door manufacturers. And then, because swing-doors do swing and often hit people, it was alleged, even more unkindly, that the committee had been of bandage manufacturers and purveyors of healing ointments. One schoolmaster, forced to introduce swing-doors into a school that had never known a fire, reported 86 accidents in one year as a result of the new safety doors, ranging from crushed fingernails to fractures. If most of us haven't suffered actual injury from such doors I'm sure we've all had near misses as the swing-back from a previous user comes hurtling our way, particularly if we're approaching the door backwards at the time, and what other way is there to approach and open such a door when you're carrying something in both hands? I'm always intrigued in any laboratory to see if they've jammed open their 'Keep Shut. Fire Doors' or not. These days people in laboratories are likely to be carrying glass, radioactive isotopes, viruses – even plague, I suppose – and the danger from swinging doors must on occasion be colossal. And certainly far greater than the danger from fire.

Bringing in a new set of fire regulations isn't just a matter of injuring a few more people, and creating a new set of hazards as doors leap at us like boomerangs. It's also a matter of money. On occasion, a very great deal of money. Take Oxford University, for example. If the University buildings are to comply with the new regulations someone will have to pay £4½ million. If the colleges are included, the total bill goes up to £14 million. A colossal

sum, and for what? If it's primarily to make Oxford safer
for students it could be argued, very easily, that the money
isn't necessary because, according to reports, only one
student has died from fire in a University building in the
past 400 years. Of course, there may be a massive fire
killing dozens of students just round the corner, and
firemen may make this point, but past history - of 400
years - is most revealing. I personally find that figure of
one student death amazing. After all, students are not
always the most responsible of individuals, and the Oxford
ones used to have coal fires in all their rooms, and surely
some pranks have led to massive fires and student
deaths; but apparently not so. However, that isn't
stopping the new regulations coming into force. If anyone
really wanted to save student life they could spend the
£14 million on stopping students killing themselves, which
they do more than most, or driving so fast and so
carelessly, which young people also do more than most.
But there's a juggernaut momentum to such things as fire
regulations. They arrive; they won't go away. And I liked
the despairing cry from Oxford's Geology Department
which said it had just had its first fire for 30 years, a fire
caused by contractors at work on implementing the new
fire regulations.

So how does such a juggernaut get going in the first
place? Well, perhaps there's a fire which attracts the
public eye. Let's say it kills a dozen pensioners in an old
people's home. There is an outcry, and a call for greater
safety. So, a commission is established with instructions
to come up with suggestions for making buildings safer.
Reasonably enough, the commission is stacked with
firemen. Their duty is to see that no one and nothing is
ever destroyed by fire. It is not to bring down fire loss to,
say, 75 per cent of its present level of death and damage.

So, because firemen hate long passages, single staircase
buildings, and combustible materials, they are happy to
suggest regulations which would - without a doubt - make
fires both less likely in the future *and* easier to put out. So
far, so good; but the juggernaut is on its way. The
insurance companies are quick to say that they won't
insure a place, such as a school or a hotel, unless it

complies with the new fire regulations. And Local
Government won't give a licence, or a grant, or even
permission – unless the new fire regulations have been
obeyed. And what kind of schoolmaster or other kind of
semi-public person can deliberately disregard fire safety
regulations? The juggernaut will crush him, even though
he may have been perfectly correct, bearing average risk
in mind, that there were better ways of spending the
money than introducing finger-pinching, body-bruising
and bone-breaking boomerangs in every passageway.

What a firemen's committee cannot bear in mind – it's
not their brief to do so – is the subsequent effect of all their
recommendations. But, inevitably, firms will be put out of
business, hotels and restaurants will have to close, profits
will be turned into losses, and even normal house-owners
who wish to put tenants in their houses may be subjected
to considerable fire-prevention cost. It's been estimated
that an ordinary two-storey London house in multiple
occupation – as the jargon puts it – needs £1,500 spent on it
to bring it into line with the new fire regulations. A four-
storey house needs £5,000. In other words, a lot of people
might decide not to initiate multiple occupation just
because of the swinging doors and so on. It was *not* the
committee's concern to worry about such things but that
doesn't stop such things from happening.

Take the important matter of stately homes, and of all
our architectural heritage. Brush aside the fact that, in a
typical year only one or two people die in a pre-1800
building other than a private house. And be equally
sweeping with the fact that most fires in old buildings are
caused by builders, renovating, using blow-lamps, setting
fire to chimneys. And disregard arson which certainly
damages a stately dwelling or two, such as Anne
Hathaway's Cottage in 1969, the eighteenth-century
Aylesbury County Hall in 1970 and the Brighton Pavilion
in 1975. Then apply the regulations. Fill up those stately
passage vistas with 30-minute fire-doors. Install smoke
lobbies where necessary and by all staircases. Make fire
stairs non-combustible. Push sprinklers through the
painted ceilings. Attach hose-pipes to the panelling. And,
hey presto, at the cost of tens of thousands of pounds, or

hundreds of thousands, one building has been saved for posterity. It's often said that the damage done by pumped water in a fire is greater than the damage the flames achieve. It seems on the cards, if not a certainty, that the damage done by fire precautions will be greater than the harm which might have been done by fires. As the Royal Fine Art Commission put it the other day, it has become 'increasingly concerned about the inflexibility with which fire regulations can be pressed by fire officers, and in consequence enforced by local authorities'.

Or perhaps the commission should count itself lucky that it's living and working now and not in some future year. Such things as regulations don't get better. They get worse in the sense of being more restrictive, more costly, more damaging. Any committee set up to investigate fires is bound to be able to think up ways in which a negligible risk can be made yet more negligible. Why 30-minute fire-doors? Why not 45-minute fire-doors? And should wood ever be allowed anywhere, unless it's treated to have the flammability of concrete? As for thatch, or paper, or cooking fat, or cigarettes – unthinkable, the lot of them. So long as one person dies from fire in any one year a fire prevention committee just cannot say that present precautions are adequate. It has to suggest greater stricture, whatever the cost. It may be blamed if its new recommendations prove to be too gentle. It will never be blamed if they are severe.

Everything gets out of hand as soon as someone permits such a new set of recommendations to become a new set of regulations. The recommenders can recommend for all they are worth, but the rest of us must never let their various wishes be rubber-stamped into law without a struggle. If we don't fight then Oxford University has to find £14 million (of presumably our money) because its buildings are so unsafe that they have killed one undergraduate in 400 years. Someone somewhere has to have the courage to say that the buildings are safe enough. We can never make anything totally safe, but only safe enough.

A final point is that it is perfectly possible to do sums. Most buildings do have a price tag. So do their contents. If by spending, say, £50 a year on the 10 million houses in the country we cut down fire damage by £500 million a year then we might be on to a good thing. To do the sum correctly we'd also have to estimate a value for each human being lost by fire but, as the doctors and the insurance companies are doing this all the time, there shouldn't be too much difficulty in arriving at a figure. So, if the fire damage and the loss of human life is lessened by a sum greater than the extra annual expenditure, we would be spending our money well. So too with our architectural heritage. Of course, every irreplaceable loss is irreplaceable, but there is usually a price tag on it somewhere. And, as the other side of that coin, it ought to be possible to estimate how much damage might be done by obeying regulations. If a beautiful stairway, for instance, is blocked in by heavy screening, that stairway is not what it was. So too a passageway blocked at intervals by swing-doors – it has also suffered a loss in value, just as if a piece of it had been burned. A vista shrunk in size is not a vista any more.

Without doubt the new regulations will lessen fires and the damage they do. Also, equally without doubt, the new regulations will do damage and will cost a lot. If the price of implementing them, both in cash paid to the builder and destruction to the building, is greater than the damage they save, then let's forget them forthwith. Firemen *must* make recommendations. It's part of their job. The rest of us can turn them into regulations or leave them well alone. That's our job.

Committees

I personally like the camel. I think it is a splendid beast, with dignity, and an implacable loathing for mankind. It can live in the heat and drought of the world's most difficult areas, and knows every trick in the trade for conserving water. Its faeces are almost dry enough to burn the moment they are extruded. Its urine can shift from eight litres a day, if food is abundant, to a miserly half a litre. It can accept weight loss with equanimity shrinking by 17 per cent in eight days if things are bad. It can travel 600 miles between watering points and can let its personal temperature oscillate by 11 degrees Fahrenheit, as yet another way of sneering at the savage environment in which it lives so well. It *is* a remarkable creature, and anyone who has ever ridden one will know that it has yet another card to play. It can make the rider sea-sick, if that is the word, almost instantaneously. What other transport animal is so remarkable?

I say all this in support of *Camelus dromedarius* because of a phrase in which the animal is implicated. It is said that a camel is a horse designed by a committee. I have tried to find out but failed to discover who originated this remark, partly because I wanted to learn from him or her their reasons and why such an excellent beast as the camel should be sneered at in this manner.

Let's think of a committee for a moment, and how it works. There are, say, a dozen people on it, but only one of them really knows about a particular subject. So, he or she outlines some plans. These are simple, clear, probably correct, and sound in design - like a horse, in fact. Someone else, who doesn't like this first person then tries to erode that simplicity.

'What a magnificent plan,' says Person B, 'but isn't person A being too clever by half? Doesn't he care about expense? Or the handicapped? Or kids?'

At once the committee is split into a Person A faction,

and a person B faction. People argue, not so much for or against the idea, but for and against the two protagonists. The battle rages, and then Person C introduces a new thought, not because it's good but to show interest and divert the major conflict. 'What,' he says, 'what about delaying the project?' Before the meeting he had no such thought. It just came to him, and then he feels he ought to support it. So there's then a C faction.

If this sounds humbug, go to a committee meeting. Listen to what the others are saying. Listen to what you are saying. Wonder why on earth they, or you, are suddenly advocating that the building should face south. Is it because you dislike the man who says it should face north? Or because you didn't understand the bit about finance or pre-stressed concrete but know about north and south? Anyway, be amazed and then be delighted that the point is argued seriously. And be half delighted when unanimous opinion subsequently agrees that west is a satisfactory compromise. If anything the committee produces a beast mid-way between a horse and a camel, say a llama.

But we seem to put great faith in committees. We are often told that a council has decided this or that, or trustees have given their blessing, and we seem to relax at such apparent good news. Had it been the director or some other form of chief who had made the decision, we are less likely to relax, more likely to resent the imposition of one other man's opinion. But, if he heads a council, and that council reaffirms his policy, we seem to give up, partly I suppose at such an apparent strength of opinion. We are also further confounded by the distinctive quality of the committee in question.

This may be the age of the common man but, if you want to serve on committees, it still pays to be uncommon. The British Museum, for instance, has 25 trustees, and these include 1 Duke, 4 Lords, 11 Sirs or Dames, and 7 Professors. The London Zoo Council has 1 Duke, 3 Lords and Ladies, 2 Honourables, and 8 Sirs. The Natural History Museum has no Trustee who isn't a Sir, a Professor, or an FRS. Of course, I accept that it's perfectly possible to be a good man, good for committees *and* to be a

Sir, or Lord, or some such. But a lot of other people are also good, and I'm just saying that, by and large, this great mass of other people finds it harder to serve on the noble committees.

It's also much harder to serve on such committees if you're pushed about money because they don't, as a general rule, pay you a cent for your trouble. They give tea and biscuits, sometimes a portly lunch, and probably expenses, but unless you can eat so much free lunch that you don't have to eat for the next couple of days the business of serving on such committees doesn't really help to pay the rent. And such service can demand a lot of time. The Royal Society Council (one Lord, 7 Sirs, and 7 Professors out of its 21 members) meets 10 times a year, and the 20 men and one woman on it may well be involved with other committees. The Zoo Council meets 11 times a year. The National Trust Council, with 51 members, meets 5 times a year. The British Museum trustees attend about 26 meetings a year. That's a lot of labour for tea, biscuits and a railway ticket.

This matter of no pay is probably a hang-over from the days when distinguished gentlemen could hardly expect to be distinguished gentlemen (and therefore to serve on committees) unless they had private incomes. The top job at the London Zoo, that of Secretary, fell vacant recently. There was a certain amount of talk about suitable candidates until it was learned that the job earned no salary whatsoever. Interest died among many likely contenders and, equally reasonably, the post went to someone who already had a job which did provide a salary. So, the Zoo ended up with someone in charge of their affairs who already had a very full-time job elsewhere.

In these days, when private incomes are far less probable, it is important for potential committee and council members to have the sort of job they can just leave without either rebuke or loss of earnings. 'Goodbye, Jane,' says the big man to his secretary. 'I've got that committee meeting with Sir John for the rest of the day. Look after my calls will you, and I'll probably be in tomorrow.' Not everyone has that kind of job, such as the young.

Therefore, the young, in general, do not have their names on the committee masthead.

The more governmental kinds of committee do tend to get paid. Each member of the Nature Conservancy Council receives £850 a year, which means some £90 a day for the 9 Council meetings. The Medical Research Councillors get £750 a year for their 9 annual meetings. The Science Research Councillors get £825 a year, unless, as with the MRC and the Nature Conservancy, they are government employees in which case they get no extra wage. This seems fair enough, as they're already getting a full-time salary and part of their job is sitting on these other councils. What is more surprising is that someone who has a full-time job, and therefore a full-time wage, is allowed to go off and sit on other committees which pay him money for *not* being at his proper desk. So, it's 'Jane, look after my calls for me because I'm away earning more money somewhere else partly because you are here to hold this particular fort for me'.

A final point is that the distinguished councils up and down the land, which do run a surprising number of our important organisations, are composed of a certain kind of person. By this, I am not referring to the sorts already mentioned, such as the aristocracy, or those who can work for no more pay, or those with a competent Jane. Instead, I am thinking of the style of person who is likely to be proposed for an important committee. He has probably done well, is mature in his outlook, is getting on in years, and has important letters after his name, or medals, or honours rewarding his career. It will all look well on the ballot paper for his election.

If I were to choose one word for such a person I would say that he or she is smug. Their future is, in the main, behind them and they have done well with their lives. They have a right to be smug. Each has earned that comfortable smile upon his face. 'Hello, Sir John. Good to see you again. Ah, there's the general. Must have a word with him, and find out what he thinks of our new managing director.' I'm not saying the less distinguished are better. But they would be different, in their outlook and temperament. So would the young, and all those still beavering to earn their

distinctions, still lean and hungry. Our important committees, by and large, are not just noble, and unpaid, and
happy to steal their clientèle from full-time occupations,
but are most uniform in their composition. They are all
much of a muchness if you study the lists involved.

I still don't think it fair to say that a camel is a
committee's idea of a horse. I would prefer the proposition
that a dodo is its idea of an eagle. Or that a manatee, so
contentedly browsing, is replacement for all the fun,
liveliness and intelligence of the bottle-nosed dolphin. The
camel is a splendid beast and, dare I say so, more amazing
than any kind of horse. I don't think that your average
committee is capable of creating such amazement. It just
looks, on paper and on the masthead, as if it could.

Christmas

Now, it seems to me, is an excellent time for taking a cool look at Christmas; for wondering if it's all that it could be, and for wondering, also, if it shouldn't go away. Before embarking upon the arguments, and imagining what a national plebiscite might reveal about our national wishes, a plebiscite with no one, of course, under the age of 18 getting a vote, it is as well to remind ourselves of the reality of Christmas.

I don't wish to knock it, at least not yet, but it is true, isn't it, that the shops are foul at this season, and increasingly so as the weeks go by? And the traffic is foul. And the country's machinery seems to come to a halt - oh, we couldn't mend your vacuum cleaner, or clean your clothes, or fix your gas, at least not until after Christmas. And it's also true, isn't it, that we do buy more junk at this time of year, allegedly for their joy (of receiving) and ours (of giving), but do they really want this picture, or that pot, and are they size 8 gloves or is it feet, and surely they can't actually hate crystallised fruits, or a set of six smoked eels, or this scent - heaven-scent it says - or that O from Cologne? The day itself isn't always, is it, the unending jollity that it's cracked up to be, with children - just possibly - over-gorged and undenied, with the television set on from dawn till - well, almost till dawn again, and there may have been joy in giving things away, those eels, that spray, but there can be less joy in receiving, can't there, that's if you hate crystallised fruits or take size 10? 'Roses,' said Ogden Nash, 'are things which Christmas is not a bed of them.'

We know all that, we say, but Christmas in England is so very - English. Whether or not we watch *The Sound of Music* from California, we do eat an American bird, stuffed with Spanish chestnuts, garlanded with potatoes from the New World, sprouts from Brussels, a plum pudding spiced from the Orient, and we sit around an alien

tree, and sing with music from Sweden about a King of
Bohemia, the one who looked out on St Stephen's Day.
And that other favourite carol, the one that interrupts
many a silent night, is as British as sauerkraut and
bratwurst.

Oh well, we say, perhaps we have imported a few extras
to jolly it along, but Christmas has always been more or
less the same, hasn't it? Well, has it? For one thing,
presents are quite an innovation. Read about the old
Christmases and no one, rich or poor, seemed to get or give
presents until Victoria was on the throne. And no one had
trees, as against yule logs and mistletoe, until Albert was
sitting beside her. And we may think it odd that
Christmas is now stretching from before Christmas Eve
until after New Year's Day; but, in fact, this *was* the ancient
custom before the Industrial Revolution began and
factory owners could not bear to part with their work-force
for such a length of time. So there used to be 12 days of
Christmas until these were shrunk to one or two. What
there never was, at least not until mid or late Victorian
times, was such a relationship between children and
Christmas. They have now taken it over, but they didn't
get in on the act, and certainly not dominate the stage,
until very recently.

Ah, well, we say to all that, it is *Christ*-mass, the holiest
day in the calendar, and is and always has been
sacrosanct for that reason. In fact, that's the most dubious
part of all. Not until the fourth century in Rome was there
any official celebration of Christ's birth at this time of the
year. Not until the end of the sixth century in England was
the day being firmly celebrated as Christ's birth-day. But
there's not a scrap of evidence that Christ was born on this
day. However, there is plenty of supposition that the early
Christians, wanting an occasion already firmly established as one of rejoicing and birth, deliberately chose 25
December as their important date because it already was
important, being the official birthday of Mithras, the very
popular god of the Roman Empire. Instead of being spoil-
sports, and taking away a festival, they merely switched
its relevance. In other words, for Christian or pagan,
either then or now, the period just after the winter solstice

has an ancient festive history, but for the pagans it's even more ancient than for the Christians. After all, it's quite a good time for a bit of relaxation. The days are at their shortest. There's not much that can be done outside. The animals that won't make it through the winter are having to be slaughtered. And the nights are not only long but suddenly, just after 21 December, give visible proof of shortening from then on. So let's carouse, and wassail, and celebrate the Saturnalia, whether it's the time of the Sun-God, like Mithras, or the Son of God. As people we need feasts, and like feasts, whatever their cause, or origin, or solid legacy.

So, after all that, to the point. Do we actually like Christmas the way it is? Would we prefer to have it otherwise? G. K. Chesterton said that tradition is a democracy of the dead. Quite right, but might we not prefer to rule ourselves; and are we, the living, necessarily so respectful of past occasion? Even if we are, Christmas is not what it used to be. It is changing, but without anyone saying how it should be changed. Do we really want a fortnight off at that time, which is the way things seem to be going, or would we rather have a couple of days then, followed by 10 days off, say in mid-February, when the winter is really getting us down and spring still seems an age away? If so, how on earth would we achieve such a happening? All we seem capable of doing is to enlarge Christmas, make it more gross, buy more gifts, congest more traffic, and add October to the list of months when people can't fix washing machines, or mend shoes, or fix drains. 'Can't do it till after Christmas,' they all say, and say so earlier every year.

There are many really positive reasons for wishing to change Christmas, or rather to contain it from further expansion. It is a time of considerable loneliness, not despite the jollity but because of it. People who are merely lonely at other times of the year can become acutely so at Christmas. Suicides and other expressions of despair are rife in the festive season. It is also an occasion of compulsory attendance at gatherings, generally family gatherings, which are not always wholly enjoyable. If such groupings wished to get together, they could easily do

so, but the extended family – extended to Aunt Florence,
cousin-by-marriage Gwynneth and once-removed Blanche –
is less important these days than it used to be. In Victorian
times, in particular, the large family was *the* circle in
which people lived. They married their cousins a lot,
partly because they had so many but also because they
saw such a lot of them. Without doubt, the importance of
the extended family is now on the wane. Also, without
doubt, we are extending Christmas and still think of it as a
family occasion, when we see Gwynneth, Blanche and Co.
for the only time in the year, and wonder – each time – why
we do so even then. There is no such family compulsion
about Easter, or what used to be the Whit weekend, or the
August bank-holiday, but there is for the holiday time
that's growing fastest of all.

What I'd like is a shorter Christmas and then, say,
Carnival like all those sensible Catholic countries.
Carnival isn't a family time, and it comes at a better
season when we need another holiday. It's got quite a
different set of traditions, for it gets people out of the home
and into the streets. It isn't a time of aggravated
loneliness; quite the contrary. It's a time of meeting
people, making new friends, destroying the isolation and
insularity of the rest of the year. There are lots of people
who hate Christmas. I have never, in Rio for example, met
anyone who didn't welcome Carnival, the thought of it
and then its actuality. The ceremony lasts for four days
when all the normal rules are broken. From the Saturday
before Ash Wednesday to the Wednesday itself is a
fantastic spectacle and fantastic joy. It's about as
different from our Christmas, with people slumped before
the television set, as could possibly be.

So, would we like something of the sort? Something
more suited to our climate? What would Londoners say, for
example, if the Serpentine was artificially frozen over, or if
Hyde Park became a colossal showground, or if traffic was
banned from all of central London for four days and
nights? Mini-efforts of this kind were made during Jubilee
year, and people seem to like street parties, and public
firework displays, and other official goings-on when the
normal rules are relaxed. It's often said that we mustn't

change Christmas because of the children, but children would be the first to enjoy some extra-curricular event, like a frozen piece of the Thames, or a roasted ox, and all the things that used to be. In any case, children are the minority. They can't have all the say, and perhaps we should remember that Father Christmas's true forebear - namely where all the stories sprang from initially - was a Carthaginian god who actually ate children, and the children themselves were the gifts.

So, if others like the idea of amending Christmas so that we can do other things at other times, I wonder how we'd go about it? A referendum? Well, referenda seem reserved for the issues that political parties care more about than mere happiness and holidays. So, what about direct action? That seems to work better these days. How did it happen that New Year's Day became a holiday? It happened because more and more people just took it as a holiday, and our legislators merely legislated something that was already happening. So, why don't we start next with Shrove Tuesday? The Rio Carnival has been called the Greatest Show on Earth. By comparison our festivities on that day are as exciting, no less and certainly no more, than getting one limp pancake stuck momentarily on to one patch of ceiling. Didn't it used to be a tremendous extravaganza, a farewell to meat, a colossal eating before the frugality of Lent? I'm not saying that over-eating is the greatest pleasure around, but I think we've trimmed the occasion excessively by abbreviating it into a few tired pancakes which may or may not leap from the frying pan into the frying pan. So, why don't we start with the Carnival, alias Mardi Gras, alias Fasching, and turn that time of year into another kind of holiday?

I think one of the reasons why we're so laggardly in not latching on to this ancient festival is because Christmas has such a grip on all our thinking. At the moment all we can do is extend that period. If that's all we can do then we deserve to slump in front of the television, with cousins Gwynneth, Blanche and all the rest slumped on either side, with roast, and then cold, and then devilled turkey to eat for days and days on end, so that by the twelfth day of Christmas we don't care a fig what our true love says to us. What she could say is: Why don't we shorten this holiday and have another one in February? Why don't we?

Time Zones

If there's one thing certain about any kid coming up to ask the time, it's that he or she says: 'Excuse me, have you got the right time?' What other time do they have in mind, and do they really care whether you're five minutes slow or fast? But babes, sucklings and others do speak wisely, from time to time, and there is a right time, a much neglected right time. It's called Greenwich Mean Time and, although it has an ancient history, it's still not THE time that I think it ought to be.

Let's start by talking about how we currently suffer vis-à-vis time. More of us are making long distance calls these days, and we're immediately face to face with the problem. Our cousin lives in Wyoming. That much we know. 'But America is behind us, isn't it?' we ask of those who are better at this sort of thing. But how much behind? For surely Wyoming is well to the west of New York, and isn't that about five hours different from us? Or is it five hours different when we're not on summer time, which we're presumably on at the moment even though it hasn't been much of a summer? And doesn't New York have daylight saving time, and does that make it four hours or six hours different from us, that's if it's five hours different from us normally, whenever normal is? Which still doesn't help about Wyoming, which is about two hours west of New York, or three or one if Wyoming also saves its daylight. In the end you call up the operator because you don't want to get your cousin out of bed, you don't want to have to get out of bed to call your cousin, and there must be a mutually convenient time. You then hear your local operator calling up a Wyoming operator to ask what the time is over there.

I've personally been very conscious of time zones, having just been around the world, calling in at Africa and Australia, and then up to Asia, and across America, and then back home. Not only have I landed before I took off, but I've seen the sun set and then rise again on the same day. Anyone crossing the date line has, if he's going westwards, a day lopped from his life that he can never recapture; or, if he goes eastwards like I did, will have two of the same day. I had two mother's days, more than enough for anyone, including mothers, and I couldn't take the second one seriously. Instead, I lay in my Los Angeles motel room waiting for the sun to set yet again on that Sunday 13 May, and could only start functioning properly when Monday eventually arrived.

Perhaps all Britons are equally intolerant of time zones because there's only one time in their country, the right time. We should spare a thought for Brazil, which has three times, or Canada, which has six, or the Soviet Union, which has 11. In short, it's all very muddling. In the old days, when hardly anyone had watches but there was a clock in the village square, everyone worked to that particular clock. That was the right time. It didn't show the same time as the next village clock, but this didn't matter and it continued not to matter until trains started running across big countries like the US and Canada. How could a time-table operate that took account of all the local clocks with every village clocksmith adjusting his time piece to be at 12 noon when the sun was, as near as eyes could squint, at its maximum altitude? So the American railways divided the United States into four time zones, and worked out their time-tables accordingly. All the village clocks then had to follow suit.

A few years later, in 1884, the Americans went further and suggested that the world in general should come to its senses about time. The meridians of longitude then in use were based on 13 different cities, and delegates met in Washington, DC, to agree on a prime meridian for everybody. Strong contenders were Greenwich (because the majority of nations followed Britain's maritime lead), Rome (because that was an ancient centre of the world), Jerusalem (for the same sort of reason), the Pyramid of Giza (because that was yet more ancient), and Paris. The French were particularly keen on Giza and Jerusalem (even though there was no observatory at either place) and the British apparently were not zealous about Greenwich being chosen. Anyway, Greenwich *was* chosen, and

Britain celebrated the event, this accolade from the entire world, with an excitement measuring about .001 on the Richter Scale. Not only did it subsequently move the Greenwich Observatory away from Greenwich to a place in Sussex about a quarter of a degree east of the meridian but, if you look around Greenwich Park for signs that this is a world-famous spot, you'll find – at least, I did when I last looked – a short plank with 'To the Meridian' painted on it in letters of peeling black. There may be something better inside the old Observatory building, but outside there's a bit of crude cast iron fixed to a brick wall that's to one side of a narrow path. The cast iron has a vertical lump running down the middle, the outward and visible sign of that compliment paid to us nearly 100 years ago when the world decided to base longitude upon us, and therefore every time zone upon this crucial, man-made and invisible great circle, the prime meridian of them all. Just think what, say, the Americans would be doing with such a possession. There'd be a mile or so of gilt-edged meridian set into the ground, and marines guarding it, and meridian hot-dogs and T-shirts, and all very different from that bit of plank and piece of iron in SE3.

At all events, the world knew thenceforth what time it was. Order had been created from the disorder of countless village clocks all chiming away in their own sweet time. So, what do we do when there is order, with even the maps showing the time zones of the world? Well, we create disorder once again. The man largely to blame was a Chelsea builder named William Willett. He died in 1915, but spent much of his life before then bemoaning the fact that we wasted so much daylight, particularly in the summer months when we all get up hours after the sun itself has risen. As a result of Mr Willett's efforts a Bill was presented to the British Parliament in 1908 which would, if passed, have initiated a form of summer time. It wasn't passed, and we stayed with Greenwich Mean Time. Mr Willett re-doubled his efforts, but died a year before daylight saving was introduced. It was the Germans who did what Mr Willett had failed to do. In 1916, in the middle of the war, they introduced a daylight saving scheme. That did it. If it was good for the Germans it must be good

for us, particularly as the French had already followed the
German lead. At least the three principal contenders
would thenceforth be fighting their war at the same time.
If either side intercepted a message saying that an attack
would begin at 6 am, no one would have to wonder if that
meant 5 or 7.

With the war's ending the daylight saving scheme was
allowed to lapse, but it was re-introduced in the 1920s. The
Second World War threw time into confusion again;
summer time was expanded to mid-November. And then
throughout the entire winter. And then double summer
time was introduced. With the war's ending, everything
changed yet again, and then *again* in 1947 when fuel was
so short, and then again in 1968 when we, of all people, got
rid of Greenwich Mean Time altogether. We put our clocks
one hour forward of GMT, and invented British Standard
Time, as if that wasn't a confusingly named alternative to
the universal standard of Greenwich time, but we've
changed our tune since then and poor old Mr Willett must
be turning in his grave, and so must all those delegates to
the Washington conference who thought they had created
order. Plainly we now have disorder because how many of
us know for sure whether we're ahead of or behind GMT at
this moment, and what time it is in France, let alone at our
cousin's place in Wyoming?

So, I'm wondering if it isn't high time that the whole
world didn't think more about Greenwich Mean Time, or
Universal Time (as the scientists call it), or Zulu as the
airlines call it. Science, aviation, navigation – they all use
a single time. They have to, otherwise no one knows what
the other person's talking about. There are extra times,
like sidereal time and ephemeral time, but for ordinary
planetary events there is and has to be standardisation of
time. And the standard used is that based on the prime
meridian, the one that goes through, among other things,
a piece of cast iron stuck to a wall just below the old
Greenwich Observatory.

What's very strange, to my mind, is that the whole
world likes to get up at about 7 o'clock – or 5 hours before
midday – and goes to bed at about 11 o'clock, or 11 hours
after midday. People don't do what the animals do,

namely get up with the sun and go to bed with the sun, or even have midday as the middle of the day. In fact, what with summer times and time zones and national frontiers, the sun may be at its maximum altitude a couple of hours earlier than when our clocks strike noon. So, not only do we not know what time it is in Wyoming, but it isn't even the right time in Wyoming.

I imagined that ships might act more wisely, if only because ships' captains know all about longitude, and are more aware of the solar zenith than most of us, and can fix the ship's time however they please. So, I called up a ship's captain and discovered that the so-called Ship's Mean Time *is* adjusted as the master thinks fit. One man, sailing through Antarctic waters, wanted his crew to be at their most alert during the night watches, and therefore adjusted the ship's noon to be around 3 am. Another captain had a cargo of tourists on board who were unaware just how hot it could get in the tropics, and who suffered heatstroke alarmingly. So, he adjusted noon on the ship's mean time and, therefore, had everybody indoors eating lunch throughout the most searing time of day.

Aren't there lessons in those tales for us? Plainly, we don't really care whether the sun is precisely overhead whenever our watches say 12 noon. The time zone business scotched all that, and the various summer times interfered still further with this very basic concept. But what we don't do is adjust our clocks to our personal advantage, like those ships' captains. Why do we wait until our Government decides that clocks should be put forward or back and then feebly follow suit, arriving at our offices by the same watch time but one hour different by the sun? The Government produces vague statements about daylight saving being good for the nation, or farmers, or milkmen, or children coming home from school; but what about us? Wouldn't we like to start a couple of hours earlier in summer, or even four hours earlier, or at least think about doing so? As I say, animals do so but we, ever since we invented the clock, seem incapable of altering our habits to the seasons. We seem to imagine that the clocks do show, as the children keep on

saying, the *right time* when they do nothing of the sort.
They just show *a* time and we follow it, precisely, abjectly
and unthinkingly.

Just suppose that everybody's watch showed Greenwich Mean Time. It would be odd for some, getting up, say,
at 9 p.m. and going to bed at 1 p.m., but this very oddness
would cause them to consider what time they should get up
and should be going to bed. Also, magically, everyone
around the world would know exactly what was meant by
9 p.m. Of course, we still wouldn't know what time was
best to call our cousin in Wyoming, and he'd still get us out
of bed when he called us, but at last the world would have a
standard time, a universal time, a time for all seasons.

'What's the right time?' the kids would ask.

Well, it's Greenwich Mean Time, isn't it, and has been
for almost a hundred years?

Travel Rights

I wonder if you've ever met a Russian? By that I don't mean some ex-Russian, some emigré now settled over here, but a current citizen of the Soviet Union. And I don't mean have you seen someone on television, such as an acrobat or politician performing in Britain? No, I mean, by this apparently daft question, have you had one in your home, or found that the fellow next to you in the pub was a Russian, or that your fellow-tourist in, say, Spain was one?

I ask this question because I have been asking it of friends recently. By and large, they haven't. If the friends are scientists, or frequent delegates to international conferences, they may well have done so; but, in the main, they haven't met Russians casually in this country, much as one meets Americans, Arabs, Greeks, Turks, or even visitors from western Samoa or Timbuctoo. It isn't as if there aren't an awful lot of Russians, over 250 million at the last count, which is more than there are Americans. It is also more than there are Turks, Greeks, Dutch, French, Belgians, Swiss, Spanish, Italians, Yugoslavs, Israelis and Austrians put together, and one has certainly met plenty of that lot. Russians may be thick on the ground around Moscow, and I remember once being taken to task for saying the population there was dense, but the ordinary people of the Soviet Union either can't or won't or just don't travel here. I will go further and say that they don't really travel to any part of western Europe to any major extent.

I say all this partly because the history of western Europe in the past 30 years or more has been - to say the least - tremendously influenced by the activities of the Soviet Union. And I say it because of a fundamental belief that people should meet each other. At the time of the last war I had not met a single German, and I think it much easier - even at this crudest level of human misunderstanding - to go

to war against another nation if you are not confused by
having friends over there, or at least acquaintances, or some
degree of relationship, however minor.

I do find it very disturbing that people of the eastern bloc
may travel within it, but the bloc is apparently unwilling for
its citizens to discover how life goes on in any other bloc. The
rules concerning foreign travel there vary from country to
country, and are frequently being revised, but no Russian,
East German, Czech, Hungarian or the others of that campus
can do what we do with such facility, namely acquire a
passport (by right), buy a ticket, get a visa from the
destination (if need be), and then go.

I have not seen the statement expressed anywhere, but
surely foreign travel from one country to another begets
travel back again. By that I mean, if you meet a
Hungarian over here, you are more likely to travel to
Hungary. Friends travel to meet friends, and each brings
their currency with them. Besides, it is not necessary to
travel with great riches. In those austere years after the
war when Britain was short of everything, including
foreign cash, the British traveller overseas was permitted
to take only £25 outside the sterling area in any single
year. That was hardly largesse and the roads of France
were lined with hitch-hiking fellow countrymen, but at
least we could get out, breathe another country's air, see
other ways of life, experience other forms of government,
and broaden our outlook on the world. Travel, said Francis
Bacon all those years ago, is 'a part of education'. It is also,
said Fanny Burney, 'the ruin of all happiness, because
there's no looking at a building here after seeing Italy'. It is
just possible, isn't it, that regimes do not wish their people
to travel because it may ruin the people's contentment?
They may not like the society they are building when they
see what has been built elsewhere.

It isn't just the eastern bloc that makes travel difficult.
Brazil, for example, could not be a more different place, but
it's also a difficult place to leave, that's if you're a
Brazilian. Not only do you have to amass sufficient funds
for your ticket and your holiday expenses, which is hardly
the fault of the government, but you have to deposit 22,000
cruzeiros with the government, which is entirely at its

request. You get this money back, this £600 or so of deposit,
but only after a year. By then, with inflation running at
about 30 per cent, it's only worth about £400. If you happen
to make one trip overseas every year you have, in effect, to
lodge £600 permanently with the government for the
privilege of doing so. If you happen to be poor, of course
you don't go anywhere. But if you happen to be rich
enough to buy a ticket you still can't go, at least not until
you've found another 22,000 cruzeiros which, in effect, is
the price of the passport. Once upon a time, passports were
documents solely to assist travellers in negotiating
foreign lands. Nowadays, more and more, they are a leave
of absence from one's own country, an exeat, a liberty
pass, a licence to travel, a reward and not a right.

Mention human rights these days, and people mention
back the Helsinki Declaration. They refer to it even more
in eastern Europe because it was an important advance
and has created a greater lenience, or rather a relaxing of
previously rigid laws. When in eastern Europe recently, I
asked for an example of what Helsinki might mean to a
normal family. 'Suppose,' they said, 'suppose a man's
father was dying in the United States. Well now, due to
Helsinki, he'd almost certainly find it easier to get a
passport for the journey. He probably wouldn't be able to
take his wife, or his son, but at least *his* chances of being
able to go are now much higher.' This may seem a modest
advance to us but, if that particular right didn't exist
before, it's a tremendous advance. So, Helsinki isn't just a
scrap of paper.

Rather ashamed that I had never seen a copy of the
Declaration, but then somewhat mollified by the fact that
friends over here were equally ignorant, I got hold of a
copy. Price 65p. from the Stationery Office it's not even
called anything to do with Helsinki. Instead it's the
Conference on Security and Co-operation in Europe.
FINAL ACT. The Conference went on for quite a while,
starting at Helsinki in July 1973, continuing at Geneva
from September 73 to July 75, and then concluding at
Helsinki again in August 75. Looking at the list of
delegates I see it was signed by every European country I
can think of, except for Albania, but I'm not sure whether

Albania signs anything. Signing for us was Harold
Wilson and he, along with Helmut Schmidt, Gerald Ford,
Pierre Trudeau, Tito, the late Aldo Moro and 29 others, put
their names at the end of its 50 printed pages. I was curious
to see whether it referred in any way to the right to normal
travel, not only when a father is dying or mutual trade is
necessary, but just to get up and go and have a look at
another country.

Well, it does do that. After a good many pages dealing
with such issues as sovereignty, the use of force, the
inviolability of frontiers, equal rights, freedom of thought
and religion, prior notification of major military manoeu-
vres, and so on - without doubt important issues every one
- it suddenly mentions the Promotion of Tourism. And I
couldn't agree with it more. It affirms that the participat-
ing states are aware of the contribution made by
international tourism to the development of mutual
understanding among peoples. It then goes on to state, in
similarly forthright terms, just how tourism might be
increased, by making frontiers less complex, having
conferences on the subject, encouraging visits outside the
peak season, and so forth.

However, there is one clause that causes me more than a
twinge of anxiety. This states that tourism should be
encouraged on both an individual and group basis.
Innocuous enough on the surface, perhaps, but I wish to
take issue with it. It's the group part that worries me. I
think it always has worried me, but it came to a head the
other day. I was in a Prague hotel, trying to get a room and
on the point of succeeding - there always does seem to be
one more room if you hang about long enough - when a
tourist bus arrived, the blatant and crowded cause of that
hotel's near total roomlessness. The visitors were Russians, and they transformed the lobby into a passable
imitation of a steerage hold within an emigrant ship
leaving Europe for the New World about 100 years ago.
Everybody had bundles, but everybody was apparently
one bundle short, and a little bit frantic. The hotel did
wonders and within three hours everybody had acquired a
room. That evening they all amassed in the lobby again,
and drove in their bus to fill up a restaurant before they

returned to occupy the lobby once more and eventually their rooms. In the morning the same scenario was run backwards, as rooms disgorged bundles, and people, and a lot of talk, until the bus received it all. That coachload had done Prague.

Of course, it had done nothing of the sort, any more than we do when we package ourselves on some trip that allegedly shows us everything. I think such compressed transportation, however cheap and simplified, is the very antithesis of travel. It permits people to pass through another land without meeting any of its citizens. It has contributed nothing to mutual understanding. Worse than that, it can permit tourists to visit other places, and return with their previous opinions untarnished by the experience for the very reason that there has been no experience. Adventure, they say, is bad planning. Very true. Let that bus break down. Be forced to accommodate all its passengers within the village of the mishap. Let them meet those locals, eat with them, attempt to speak with them. 'Travelling,' said Descartes, 'is almost like talking with men of other centuries.' Not talking with people is, to twist that phrase a bit, not even travel of any kind.

So, I won't cheer should I see a busload of eastern Europeans being driven through England and cocooned against all significant happening. But I will cheer very loudly should I discover, thanks to Helsinki or any other cause, that the person next to me in the pub is Russian. He may not like the beer, and it may cost me a packet filling him up with vodka, but at least we will have met. And that, I believe, must be better by far than all 250 million of them staying over there.

Names

One definition of IQ is the number of seconds that pass before someone uses the pronoun 'I' in a sentence. Film starlets are said to score three on average and even some of one's best friends don't score much more. But *I* am about to compound this particularly egocentric frailty, for *I* am going to talk about Anthony Smith, or rather about the snags of being a smith of any sort, let alone A. Smith, a kind of non-name if ever there was one. There are over 81,000 people called A. Smith in England and Wales alone, and there are certainly scores of Anthony Smiths – I once knew of five working for the BBC.

There doesn't seem to me to be much point in having a name that doesn't do its job, that doesn't identify you. Of course, there are times when we don't wish to be identified, and I remember once when my hotel caught fire. We all hurried into the street, and there had to be quite a serious roll-call to discover if anyone was still inside. A sudden vision of *everyone* being called Smith flashed before my eyes. In fact, I was the only Smith but there were *six* Joneses. So, times have changed. But, for the most part, we don't wish to be anonymous. Our names are useful. We find them useful, our friends do so, and so does society as a whole. So, I'm wondering if it mightn't be a good idea for everyone to have a unique name, a name that is his or hers, and his or hers alone.

After all, horses do it, by and large. There may be scores of Black Beauties cantering about privately, but as soon as a horse is to be a public figure, and run races and jump officially, its name has to be registered. Not only must this name be no longer than 18 digits, including the spaces, but it must not duplicate the name of any existing horse. You just can't call your new foal Red Rum, however much you like the name, and however much it may be out of Red River and by Rum and Coke. The other Red Rum still lives, and so possesses that name exclusively. In fact, with famous horses, such as those that have won classic races, they keep the name even after death. Plainly, there is scope for confusion if a new Red Rum steps on to the scene the moment the other one has died.

So too, more or less, with dogs, goats and actors, to name but a few. A goat, for example, cannot have a registered name longer than 13 digits, and an Equity member cannot have a name already possessed by another Equity member. Just as it could be confusing to have two Billy Wonders in the goat world, so would it be troublesome to have two Laurence Oliviers on stage. So, I'm wondering if the rest of us can't catch up with, for instance, the horses, dogs, goats and actors? Why can't we have individual names?

The fact that we don't has led us into a plethora of numbers. We have so many numbers that we can't remember one of them. There's our national insurance number, and our passport number, and bank account number – that's if you can read those hieroglyphics which are written by or for computers. We have a tax number, and a VAT one if we're registered, and a car number, and as for our driving licence that's got three numbers on it, with just one of them being 19 digits long. Everybody likes to give us a number, a different number, whether it's for a cheque card, a credit card, a building society, a TV licence, or even a dog licence, and of course we can't remember them. But *they* have to give *us* numbers because our names aren't good enough.

So, where did names go wrong? After all, they have always existed to identify us, but now fail to do so. It seems that things first started going wrong after the Norman Conquest. Before then there had been lots of Old English personal names in use, but it became increasingly the thing to do to take a Christian name so favoured by the Normans, and only a few of these names were popular. The use of surnames then became increasingly common to prevent such confusion, and by the end of the fourteenth century practically everyone in England had a hereditary surname.

So, names were good and then surnames were better, but

today they're not good enough. It isn't just the joke names
of Smith, Brown and Robinson that can make one despair
when looking through the phone book in London. There
are even 17 whole columns of Patel, that name so favoured
on the Indian continent, and there's quite an assortment
of Chang, said to be the commonest surname in the world
as it's possessed by 10 per cent of all Chinese.

Therefore, what's to be done? It seems to me that there
are two possibilities. One is to make our names unique.
The other is to give us a single number, good for
everything, much as they do in the services, and I must
say that I prefer the former. I don't see what's wrong with
names, and with making them do the job they are
supposed to do. But, like horses and goats, and doubtless
important pigs and cows, there'd have to be only one
individual for each name. We could change our Christian
names around a bit, but it's probably easier to tamper with
our surnames, and a few people seem to have had this
bright idea. For example, there are 39 columns of Jones in
the London phone book which are preceded by a single
entry for Joneidi. There are 75 Smith columns, but just one
Smiter entry. Also, one should never forget P. G.
Wodehouse's Psmith, nor all those people who so disliked
the name Smith that they got rid of it altogether, such as
Sugar Ray Robinson, Marty Wilde, P. J. Proby, Trader
Horn, and Mary Pickford. Running contrary to this trend
was Dodie Smith who, until she saw the light in 1935,
actually used the pen-name Anthony Smith, as if there
weren't enough of them.

But a lot of people get attached to their surnames and
don't want to change them. It may have been all right for
David Daniel Kominsky to become Danny Kaye, and for
John Henry Brodribb to become Henry Irving, but most of
us seem to like our family name because it *is* our family
name. And what's good enough for our father should be
good enough for us. So, perhaps it's a better idea to think of
changing our first names, and improving upon the rather
limited supply. Apparently, and according to a book called
First Names First, the Smiths of this world have not been
unwilling to dream up exciting first names to go with their
boring second names. There has been an Aesop Smith,

an Amorous, an Ark, a Bonus, a Brained, and a Bugless,
a Clapham, a Christmas Smith, and what a good idea. Or
rather, what a lot of good ideas, so that everyone else can
know which Smith they're talking about. There have even
been Smith Smiths.

But, just as there's an unwillingness to jettison a
perfectly good family name, however common, there's
also a reluctance to move away from conventional first
names which are, after all, Christian names. And it's often
thought unfair to saddle a babe with Clytemnestra, or
Goliath, with St Valentine or Uz, as others have done. So,
with first *and* last names somewhat fixed in our minds,
what's wrong with changing our middle name? They're
nothing like so precious, and I don't see why John Uz
Brown should feel resentful, any more than Jane Clyte
Smith. They're still John Brown and Jane Smith, but
should they wish, they can raise themselves from the base
line by remembering their Clyte and their Uz. Harry S.
Truman, American president, had much the same done for
him by his parents. They made him unique because that S.
is just an S. and stands for nothing at all. Mr and Mrs
Truman couldn't decide between the two grandparental
names of Solomon and Shippe, and opted for S. instead.

If we did all have unique names, and had first to check
whether there was another John Uz Brown before we
attached this handle to our little one, I wonder if the
Government and all its quango offspring would cease to
give us numbers? They do seem obsessed with numbers
and I wonder, if these are so vital, why we can't just have
one of them? And to have it shorter than is generally the
case? As there are only 50 million of us in this country, no
one's number need be more than 8 digits long.

Better still we could have letters. As there are 26 of them
as against only 10 kinds of numeral, our unique
assortment of letters could be shorter. In fact, if no one's
identity was to be more than seven letters long, like MNX
PRS T, there's room for everyone in the world to be
included in a seven-letter system. Twenty-six letters to the
power of 7 is far greater than the total world population.
But it's difficult to remember seven letters in a row. So, we
could get back to that old telephone system that they had

in London and other major cities of three letters followed by four figures. We can remember those very easily, and I still can't forget scores of the old phone numbers. In fact, a combination of three letters followed by four figures is not only easy to remember, it's also something that provides over 175 million different arrangements, starting off with ΛΛΛ 1111 and going right through all the possible combinations.

A dread thought strikes me that this might imperil liberty in some way, that computer operators could check on our medical record by knowing our bank account number, and vice versa. There would have to be safeguards against that possibility, but I don't think it's beyond the wit of modern man to think them up. Anyway, I don't really like the idea of numbers at all, whether just numbers or combinations of letters and numbers, when we've all got names. I still wonder why we can't use them – for everything. Making them unique, particularly when we have a middle name to play with, would not be difficult. The actors do it. The goats do it. And we could do it so very easily. Certainly the people to start it are those called Smith, the daftest name of all in the western world, of whom the A. Smiths are the most daft. That is unless they are called Aesop Smith, Albino Smith, Amorous Smith. Well, if I want to be unique, I can't have any of those. So, let's just say I'm pondering the problem. Aescalus? No, too difficult to spell. Amaryllis? Too complicated. Ant? Could be. Anthony Q. Smith. Yes, quite a possibility. Anyway, I am working on it. What's in a name? Nothing if it's shared by thousands of others. It should be one's very own.

Godparents

I would rather that nine particular people did not hear this broadcast. I feel fairly safe with three of them, as they live in Australia, Geneva and Verona, but the remaining six live here and just might be listening. So, I hope they've found something else to do as I wouldn't like them to be reminded – yet again – of my failings towards them. The reason I am so concerned about Karen, Nicholas, Nigel, Katie, Spray, Francis, Gervase, Dominic and Jo is that I was given a special status by their parents. I don't think I have fulfilled that role very well, but then I was never quite sure what I was meant to do. You see, for every one of those children I was appointed as a godparent.

The parents themselves were, in the main, vague about any definite duties. They even brushed aside the offer that every birthday and Christmas should be marked by some godparental gift. And they were adamant that any role, however distinct and undefined, would come to a halt when the babe in question reached the age of 21. It always strikes me as ludicrous that any babe, mewling, puking and worse in its mother's arms, is ever going to stand on its own two feet, let alone reach the distinguished age of 21, but I liked the idea of whatever it was that I wasn't doing coming to an end.

Sometimes, complete with the relevant infant clad in an ancient robe that grew markedly more ancient with every burp, I and the parents and others stood around a font for the ceremony. I liked this service, for it seemed to smack of Salisbury Plain and centuries long since gone, but the words were awesome. The Church knew well enough what godparents had to do, and said so in its exhortation. 'For as much as this child hath promised by you his sureties to renounce the devil and all his works, to believe in God and to serve him; ye must remember that it is your parts and duties to see that this infant be taught, so soon as he be able to learn, what a solemn vow, promise, and profession, he hath here made by you. And that he may know these things the better, ye shall call upon him to hear sermons; and chiefly ye shall provide that he may learn the creed, the Lord's prayer, and the 10 Commandments, in the vulgar tongue, and all other things which a Christian ought to know and believe to his soul's health, and that this child may be virtuously brought up to lead a godly and a Christian life ...'

In my case, even when we had stood in church, the parents were quick to affirm afterwards that I didn't really have to renounce the devil, that I could carry on as normal, and they didn't expect their child – now happily chewing at the costly lace around its neck – would want to do all those things, in the vulgar tongue or otherwise. But none of the 18 parents involved told me with any precision what I ought to do. They removed the lace now choking their offspring, beamed a smile at it and me, and someone took a photograph. The ceremony was ended.

However, I always had a vague thought that I would come into my own – as a godparent – should some fearful accident overtake the natural parents. I would step in, *in loco parentis*, and start doing work of real importance, instead of giving presents and head pats. I would, in short, look after the children.

Well, I would, in short, do nothing of the kind. Godparents have no status whatsoever in the eyes of the State. They are neither blood relatives nor are they a vital part of the child's settled background and both, in the eyes of any court, are far more important than some distant, avuncular, friend of the family who turns up at present-giving time and either has or hasn't renounced the devil. I had thought that the parents themselves were reluctant to say that godparents should look after their children when they, the parents, died, for the reason that people, particularly young married couples, are unwilling to face up to that most dread realisation of them all. So, in my opinion, it was left unsaid but was understood by all concerned. The godparents would be the parents in the event of an accident. But not so. Not at all.

Society, in general, still thinks that blood is far thicker than anything else, that relations should look after the children, and the nearest relations are best of all. So, if parents do nothing and there are no obvious dwellings for their bereaved children to move into, they will go to the house of a brother or sister probably, however much the parents disliked one or loathed the other. Just think for a moment, if you have infant children, where they would go if the two of you died. That aunt? That brother-in-law? Are they the people you wish to bring up your little ones? It certainly won't be the godparents, however generous with gifts, however amiable.

Most children, upon the death of their parents, are re-housed amicably. Someone takes them in and there is no dispute. It is not necessary to go to court to accept the custody of a child. The courts are happy for people to settle things themselves, to take in children where there's need; and the courts only become involved when there is dispute, as two or more persons claim custody. As every case is unique it's difficult to generalise about court decisions, but these days it is the welfare of the child that gets prime consideration. If one claimant is thought more suitable for the child, that claimant gets the custody. There is no pecking order for relations, in that brothers, for example, have a greater claim than, say, aunts or nephews. In a recent case a mother was manslaughtered by her husband. With her dead and the husband in prison there remained the problem of the children. A brother of the husband claimed them; so did a cousin. The brother, the closer relative, was thought to be far less suitable and the cousin got the custody.

Even natural fathers are getting shorter shrift these days. Suppose there is a divorce and the children stay with the mother. Suppose that mother marries again. Should she die, and should both the natural father and the step-father claim the children, the courts are far more likely to let the children stay with the step-father in their home and settled background than have them shifted to some other home and some other circumstance. In other words, genes are not what they used to be.

Amazingly, most parents make absolutely no provision for the children should they both die. Or, if they do make a will, they worry much more who is going to get what

money there is than who is going to get their children. But
the will is the easiest place to arrange for the custody of
one's children. Instead of dying intestate, so there is
possibility of feud over the money and the children, it is
plainly not idiotic to appoint a guardian and settle the
matter of custody, once and for all. These so-called
testamentary guardians don't have to be your nearest, or
your dearest, any more than those who receive your
money.

Which all brings me back to the matter of godparents.
I'm wondering if the two roles, that of guardian and of
godparent, can't be amalgamated? On the one hand are
godparents who don't really know what they should be
doing, and on the other is the very vital role of guardian, a
role that is absolutely clear should orphans suddenly be
created. If the godparent was also stated to be the
guardian, whether in the will or any other document, I feel
quite sure that the godparent would take his or her job
more seriously. Instead of just appearing with presents
and pats he or she would probably make more certain that
he or she knew more about the child in question.

Of course, there would have to be a lead godparent, so to
speak, the first in line for guardianship. But there's
nothing difficult about that. The godparental pecking
order could be understood right from the start, and could
be changed by the parents as events changed. Many
godparents are appointed when still unmarried, and
plainly their status as potential guardians changes as
they do get married, or have a child, or have so many
children that more might break their back. People change
their wills as their lives and wealth change. And it would
be good to have a pool of godparents to draw on, and one or
other of them would hold the key role as the years passed
by.

I certainly would have been glad to take in Karen,
Nicholas, Nigel, Katie, Spray, Francis, Gervase, Dominic
or Jo had ill-fortune come their way. But, alas, I would
have no right to do so, being merely a friend of the family
and neither a relative nor a testamentary guardian. So,
most of them got the odd present from time to time, and
some did better than others, but all – I feel – would have

done better by far had there been some solid civic purpose in my appointment. So, my apologies to you, that's if any of you nine are listening, but why not wonder about the godparents you may choose, and wonder if they would be good as guardians. If so, may I humbly suggest you make them guardians as well. For one thing, I'm sure your children would get more presents.

Eating Meat

Suppose, for a moment, that you and your family were to be given your share of the British Isles, and were told to get on with it, to produce the food you need to keep yourselves alive. Suppose – because this might make it easier for you to imagine – your entitlement was an island. If there are six of you in your family, your island would be about six acres in size as that would be your fair share. Of course, you'd build a house, but that wouldn't be very big for just the six of you, and you'd still have almost all of your six acres left for growing food.

So, what would you grow if you had to be self-sufficient? Well, if you were wise, you'd grow a variety of different foodstuffs, much as an allotment holder does, and you'd probably have a pig or two to eat scraps and refuse, and you'd have chickens to pick the place clean of insects and seeds and anything left behind by the pigs. But would you have a cow or sheep on your modest piece of land? They both not only need grass to eat, which would use up some of your precious acres, but would need other crops grown specifically for them to supplement their summer diet and tide them through the winter. So, on the whole, you'd probably decide against a cow or a sheep, and you'd certainly be right.

The trouble with cattle, and sheep, in fact with meat producers, is that they are very inefficient creators of protein and food value. Of course we like meat but we also like forgetting the fact that it's a wasteful way of producing what we need. The six of you on your island would be foolish if you imported a cow. But we, all of us, on our bigger British Isle, have lots and lots of cows and sheep and pigs, and they use up most of the available space. There are about 50 million people here and, as it happens, there are about 50 million cows, sheep and pigs. They, broadly speaking, occupy six times as much space as we do. If it's space that you hanker after, and you don't

like tower blocks, compressed living, crowds, and the
elbow of your fellow man, you'd be better off as a cow or a
sheep or even as a pig. They roam the acres; we pack
ourselves into the towns. So, I am wondering if we all
realise the price we pay for meat, not in pounds and pence,
but in acres, in lack of space for us. People are crowded,
cows are not, and I find that very odd. We, not they, are
herded like cattle.

Let's remember, at the start, a remark we've all heard a
thousand times or more that a piece of development has
meant the 'loss of some good agricultural land'. This new
factory will take 20 acres, a 'loss to British agriculture'.
This new housing estate, where a couple of thousand
people are to live, will destroy an entire farm, another loss
for Britain. So, how much land has been taken from
British agriculture in recent years? The answer is about
120,000 acres a year. Some half of that figure goes to new
forestry and woodland, while the other half goes to us, for
new houses, factories, roads, parks, and every other use. As
of now, we live on, work on, drive over and play on almost
five million acres. The cattle, sheep and pigs grunt over, moo
over, root over, and chew the cud over some 30 million acres.

But the situation is actually even more severe because
that leg-room for the cattle only represents the grass they
stand on. I appreciate that they eat the stuff, but they also
eat a sizeable proportion of our other crops, such as a third
of the wheat we grow, three-quarters of the barley, three-
quarters of the oats, as well as virtually all of the fodder
crops, such as turnips, mangolds, rape, kale, maize and so
on. In short, you need a lot of land to keep a cow, and you'd
be daft on your little island to do so, what with the grass,
and the cereals, and all the fodder to keep your animal
going. On the larger island of the United Kingdom not
only is half of it grazing of one sort or another, but about 70
per cent of the arable land is dedicated to producing food
for animals. Therefore, just as it's stupid and bovine for
you and family to keep a cow on your little island, so is it
odd for the rest of us to do so, to keep 13 million cows, and 7
million pigs, and 28 million sheep.

So, if you're beginning to think, as I am, that we do pay a
very great deal for our meat – in terms of space – then what

ought we to do? I suppose one possibility is to make certain
that cows live like we do, in flats, and apartments, in
multi-storey tenements, in the sort of conditions that
consume less space. Of course, they wouldn't be able to get
at grass, but for much of the year they get supplementary
food as it is, and I suppose they could live for all the year
on supplementary food, but that would mean even more of
our grain going their way, even more fodder, and also a lot
of expense in all that housing. Making cows live like
humans would undoubtedly give humans more room, so
that humans could live more like cows and have an acre or
so each, and this idea of cow cities does have appeal. After
all, most pigs and chickens already live indoors in what the
farmers call humane conditions, which I suppose means
human conditions, and the cattle might be induced to follow
suit, but they would still demand great quantities of food.
They would still, for that is the nature of meat producers, be a
costly way of producing food, in terms of acreage, of finance,
and of food to make their food, the meat we eat.

Ah, we all say, but what about protein? We need protein,
and meat is a crucial source of it. Which is, of course,
rubbish. We need protein, assuredly, just as we need fats,
carbohydrates, minerals, vitamins and water, but it
doesn't really matter where our protein comes from. It so
happens that meat is one source, a very good source, but
there are lots of other protein providers and they should
never be forgotten.

Nor should it be forgotten that it takes many more acres
to produce a gram of protein via meat than to produce
protein in almost any other way. For example, the number
of people who can be fed per acre with the protein they
require is four if the crop grown on that acre is wheat. The
number of people to receive the right protein amount
would go up to eight if the crop was potatoes, the much
despised spud. But as soon as that same acre is given over
to animals, or animal products, then the number of people
who could get the protein they need goes right down. If the
acre was dedicated solely towards milk production, not
even one person would get the protein he or she needed.
And if that acre just produced beef, then only half a person
would be protein-satisfied.

In other words, to chew the same facts on the other side of one's mouth and see them from another angle, it would be possible for the present UK population to become self-supporting in food. It would get rid of the cow and dedicate all those millions of acres to some crop that would produce far more food, far more protein, than the cow is ever able to do. Currently we produce about half our food needs. But currently we have 50 million cattle, sheep and pigs whose existence here is preventing us from becoming self-sufficient. In fact, if we forgot about meat, there'd not only be self-sufficiency but space left over for us to use, for parks, for recreation areas, or just for wilderness.

So far I haven't mentioned the protein-rich crops, such as the kind of beans that keep South Americans alive, partly because to mention soya, for example, can have us all rushing back to meat, and forgetting about the cow's intrinsic wastefulness. But there's no reason why vegetable products can't taste every bit as good, and as varied, and as exciting as meat. Go to China or Japan, for instance, where they turn practically everything into amazing kinds of food. Go to India. And then wonder again if good cooks can't work wonders with virtually any kind of raw material. They don't have to start with meat, but they've got very used to starting with it – at least in our society – and they've got very used to making it taste fantastic. But, just as a bad cook can destroy the very best of beef, so can a good one enhance just about everything, with strange sauces, herbs and oils, the right degree of punishment by fire, and expertise. After all, we are omnivores. We can eat virtually everything that isn't grass and too cellulose-rich for our digestion, but we seem to think that meat is somehow optimum. It may taste good, but at a price.

Therefore, next time you pass a herd of cows, while you are herded onto a motorway, remember the amount of space they each demand. Remember the crops we also have to grow for them. Remember that they don't have to live in blocks of flats. And that they cause the import of a lot of grain, which can come from countries that really need the stuff. Then have some delicious oriental food that makes no use of meat at all. In fact, remember the parable

of the prodigal son, and think of the calf as always far
more prodigal, as it consumes space, grass, and all
manner of supplementary foods just because we fancy
meat. You wouldn't fancy it on your little family island.
You couldn't afford to.

Japanese Road Deaths

There are quite a few cities in the world where, if you're that way inclined, you can go and watch an accident happen. Just get on the road, drive about a bit, and before too long there'll be a smash, if not before your very eyes, at least near enough for you to see exactly who did what to whom. If this is your particular pleasure may I recommend Rio de Janeiro where you should see one within 15 minutes at the most. Or Mexico City which also scores well in this event. And, until recently, I would also have recommended Tokyo. In its haste to catch up with, and then overtake, the rest of the world its drivers followed suit. The damage they did was a great boost to their burgeoning motor industry as replacements were called for up and down the land.

But things today are very different and the Japanese who have astounded us from so many points of view can also amaze us in the way they have cut down their death on the road. We in Britain go on killing about as many people, give or take a thousand, as we have always done. Even back in 1926, when national casualty figures were first collected by the police, and when very few people owned cars, we managed to kill nearly 5,000. In 1935, round about the time when Hore Belisha was bringing in his beacons, we were killing 6,500 a year. During the war, when headlights were all but covered up and you were quite likely to find an unlit tank around the corner, we killed rather more, roughly 8,000 to 9,000. There was a slump after the war, when nobody drove anything much, but we were up to 5,000 by 1959, then up to 7,000 between 1965 and 1974, and now we're down in the 6,000s. In other words, and during the past 50 years of happy motoring, we have been very consistent, killing between 5,000 and 9,000 every year, despite the blackout, a lack of cars, or a plethora of cars, and tons of new laws, speed limits, MOTs, driving licences, zebras and pandas, winking lights, seat belts, crash helmets, white lines, cats' eyes, and all sorts of different cars. It would seem as if 5,000 to 9,000 dead is the sort of price we're content to pay, somewhere between 14 and 24 each day.

So, over now to Japan and what they've been doing. Of course that country isn't quite the same as ours, because it's got twice as many people, and a different style of road network, but what they've been doing is interesting, nonetheless. Throughout the 1970s, for example, they have had more traffic on the roads every single day, and yet have steadily cut down on death. The numbers killed over the past seven years have been 16,000, 15,000, 14,000, 11,000, 10,000, 9,000 and 8,000. In this one decade they've halved their number of victims and yet the number of drivers has gone up in that time, and the number of cars has gone up, and the number of miles driven.

So, what's the difference between them and us, apart from the fact that they're wiping the floor with us industrially, and work hard, and are troubled by an excess of foreign money? Do they just care more about the inefficiency of having drivers drive into each other, and believe they should tackle the problem, just as they tackled motorcycles, cameras, motor cars, hi fi equipment, television sets, steel, shipping, and the rest? The short answer is that they did tackle it and in a way which I'm not certain we would wish to follow. Anyway, on to some facts, and then we can decide whether we like the idea of copying what the Japanese have done.

Let's start with getting a driving licence. In Japan you can go to a government driving school. That involves about 30 driving lessons and costs you £500. If you're an older man or a woman of any age, it'll cost you rather more because they say, and I'm not getting involved in this argument, women and older men are less skilled and need more training. You can go to a cheaper, private driving school, but you're then given a far stiffer test by the authorities and most people settle for the £500 government training. You also have to renew your driving licence after three years, and you're expected to take another course before you get your renewal. As the regulations phrase it: 'All drivers cannot be expected to be fully aware of new skills and knowledge answering to changes in laws and regulations and traffic conditions'. It doesn't seem to be absolutely compulsory to submit to these refresher courses and tests, but it's the next best thing as 98.3 per cent of the people do so. And they have to pay for the privilege of being brought up to date.

Just as it is hard for the Japanese driver to get a licence, it is also easy for him or her to lose it. Basically, all traffic offences, from the trivial to the major, operate on a points system. The more points you acquire the more certain it is that you will have your licence revoked, and you can acquire points for almost any sort of infringement. For example, it's 1 point for not having a tail light, 2 points for failing to observe a traffic light, 2 points for not stopping where it says Stop, 6 points for going more than 15 miles an hour above the speed limit, 8 points if you haven't got the right kind of licence, and 12 points for drunken driving. You can also pick up points by being involved in an accident, getting 9 points in a fatal accident if you were partly to blame and 13 points if you were mainly to blame. It's very easy to pick up a whole load of points, opening a door stupidly, not going fast enough on the minimum speed roads, having too many passengers, not dipping lights, carving someone up, not letting buses pull out, parking wrongly, not indicating that you're going to overtake – all of which are one point each. Therefore, mere carelessness can get you just as many points as causing a fatal smash. Collecting points isn't something to brag about down at the wrestling club as they can swiftly lead to disqualification. Get 35 and you can't drive for three years, and don't forget you can score this number of points quite easily without being involved in a single accident.

A further hazard of not obeying the rules, and having your licence suspended for a while, is that you have to go through another set of lectures. As the rule book says: 'The course is a positive corrective education aimed at fully correcting erroneous knowledge and skill'. In the past year 1,560,000 Japanese had to be taught about the error of their motoring ways, and all those who finished the course had the time of their driving licence suspension suitably shortened. In fact, it's hard getting away from all this education even if you haven't done anything. There are 15,000 Children Traffic Safety Clubs in the country, over 4,000 Traffic Boys Groups, over 10,000 Traffic Safety Meeting Groups within homes and clubs for the aged, and thousands more safety clubs at places of work.

What they're trying to do in Japan is to put the business of driving a car on a higher plane. They did have a shocking accident rate and they have instituted draconian measures to deal with it. Japan is now a nation of polite drivers, of better drivers, of safer drivers. You're quite likely to have a well-dressed drunk, complete with snazzy brief-case, cannon into you on the pavement but the chances of seeing a drunken driver are very small indeed.

So the question is: would we like all that? Would we like to pay £500 to get a licence in the first place, have to take refresher courses every three years, suffer spot checks, attend more lectures because one brake light was out of commission for too long, have our exhausts examined every six months, pay handsomely to have our cars checked every two years, and more handsomely every passing year, and forever suffer the likelihood of losing our licence?

Would we like stiffer MOT tests? Going through the indignity, expense and time of new tests, practical and theoretical, every three years? And keeping our cars in tip-top condition instead of having them scrape through the MOT once a year at our friendly neighbourhood garage? And would we like the police to be more diligent, jumping on us for each minor infringement that they saw, such as being a bit late in realising that was the turn-off, or carving someone up by mistake, or failing to dip a light? Wouldn't we tell them to go and catch burglars or jump in the reservoir?

Or – and this, of course, is the crunch question – do we consider that killing 18 a day, the current average, is about right? It would be irritating, and expensive, and time-consuming, would it not, to kill fewer people. It is fairly irritating, and costly, and tedious obeying the laws that we do have, suffering those initial tests, seeing cars become more expensive for safety reasons, having them checked officially. Of course no Minister of Transport can say that killing 18 a day is about right. But that's what we seem to say as a nation as we resent each new piece of legislation. In these days of secret ballots I wonder what answer we would give. Stricter laws like those of the Japanese which would bring down the death rate? Or the laws we have and 18 deaths a day?

Cancer

I remember the late J. B. S. Haldane publishing a poem called *Cancer's a funny thing* a few weeks before it killed him. Not many of us have that kind of courage, to joke about the disease that's to be the death of us, and even those of us who still have healthy bodies don't think of cancer as the number one subject for a good laugh. Although it only kills a sixth of us, and we should in fact be much more worried about failures in blood circulation, there is something particularly dread and fearful about cancer. So if it's your switch-off subject, then switch off now.

That said, there are oddnesses about cancer which I feel are funny, but funny peculiar rather than the other kind. For instance, I do find it odd that we, as a people, like to fly in the face of all the evidence and actually believe that a cancer cure is just around the corner. We also like to believe that enormous strides have been taken in recent years, and that we today are much better off with regard to this disease than were, say, our parents or our grandparents. Well, both beliefs need a bit of looking into and, as a start, I'll quote from a recent article by the head of an Imperial Cancer Research laboratory. To the question: Are we better off now? he answers: For each age group each of us has about the same overall probability of dying from non-respiratory cancer as had our parents, while our chances of dying from respiratory cancer – lung cancer – are far greater. As for the future, when did he think there would be a specific cure for any major form of cancer? His answer was not for another 50 years or so.

Moreover, it was his opinion that 'the public should be made to realise that most cancer research is not yet directly concerned with searching for a cure but rather for an understanding of the disease. Indeed, the prospect of such a cure seems so remote that it does not enter even into the speculative day-to-day conversation of the people who do cancer research'. I am quite certain that is not the impression of the ordinary man in the street, and I wonder if it's the opinion of those who give money to the cancer charities. In fact, I would like to know if we would behave differently vis-à-vis cancer if this fact were better known, whether we would give more money to cancer research, or less?

The reason we believe that a cure is around the corner, that miracles have already been achieved, and that our chances of 'licking the Big C', as John Wayne said, are good today is partly because we read, again and again, of tremendous advances in cancer research, of miracle cures, of steady improvements in the morbidity statistics. It would seem almost as if we are living in one of those societies where opinions are moulded for our own good, and where we worry less about cancer because we are told of victories from time to time. So what has really been achieved since cancer research began, and how is the war going?

Although research of a kind began in the last century, those were the dark ages so far as biological research was concerned. Too little was known about everything for cancer research to have much of a chance. So it's easier, and a bit more reasonable, to say that it began about 1930. Anyhow that's a useful year to start with as there's a famous current statistic, frequently quoted, which affirms that 1 in 5 cancer victims survived then for 5 years whereas 1 in 3 now survive for 5 years. Some of us might think that survival improvement from 20 per cent to 33 per cent isn't such a big deal for half a century of research, but unfortunately even that modest claim can be questioned. People will seem to be surviving longer if their cancers are diagnosed earlier, and undoubtedly there is earlier diagnosis today than there was in 1930.

What has definitely happened in the past 50 years of considerable importance to cancer sufferers is that their pain can be reduced, their operations can be handled better, and antibiotics can help diminish many of the subsequent effects of getting cancer. But cutting out a large intestine or a uterus, however smooth the operation, however absent the bacterial infection, and however

modest the pain, is hardly an advance in the compre-
hension of cancer. It may help to save the patient's life, but
it's no more a cure than cutting off a leg is a cure for
gangrene or bad circulation. It's not what everyone is
talking about when they talk of a cancer cure.

However, there have been other advances. For example,
Hodgkin's disease – a cancer of the lymph glands – used to
be invariably fatal, but a patient's chances now are better
than 50 per cent, which is encouraging for the 800 or so
who, in Britain, get this cancer in any year. And there are
various others, such as Burkitt's lymphoma and a variety
of leukaemia, which can also be treated well today.
Unfortunately, these are the rarer cancers. Against the
800 Hodgkin's sufferers must be set the 100,000 or so who
die from all forms of cancer each year in Britain. The big
cancer killers are, in general, the big killers they used to be.
There are some 200 different kinds of the disease, and
there have been some ups and downs – lung cancer going
up, stomach cancer going down – but cancer is still the
major killer that it was when cancer research began. For
people between 45 and 64 years old it is today the Number
One killer of them all.

In short, we haven't done too well in conquering this
particular assault upon our persons, and it doesn't look as
if we're going to triumph for quite a while. There is no
great cancer cure just around the corner, according to
the experts, and it won't just vanish in the way that
smallpox went, cured once and for all. So, if we can't cure
cancer, not for quite a while, what about preventing it?
This is where, in my opinion, people behave very oddly.
They long for a cure, and loathe the disease, but when
they're told that it can be prevented they disregard this
fact. For how else can we explain the relentless enthusiasm for smoking cigarettes? The smokers like the habit,
and it is an addiction, but it is odd that these two factors
are sufficient to overcome all the loathing, and fear about
cancer. If people were to stop smoking, this one change
would affect the statistics far more dramatically than the
cancer researchers have been able to achieve for all their 50
years of searching for a cure.

But smoking isn't the only thing to cause cancer. It's

generally reckoned that most kinds of cancer are caused
by our way of life. Scientists argue whether it's 70 per cent,
80 per cent, or even 90 per cent, but there is overall
agreement that most cancers in the advanced nations
could be prevented if people changed their style of living.
It's possible to make this assertion solely because people
in different areas, and living different life-styles, do suffer
from cancer in differing proportions. The Japanese, for
example, have a tremendous incidence of stomach cancer.
But move them to the United States, change their mode of
life, and they get far less stomach cancer but, unfortunately, they then get much more colon cancer. So, there
must be something in their Japanese way of life, as
against their American way of life, that causes so much
cancer of the stomach. If they were to be moved on yet
again, and perhaps become Mormons in Utah, they would
probably suffer less from all cancers in general: stomach,
colon, the lot.

It *is* our environment that largely determines how much
of what kind of cancer we're going to get as a population.
And it isn't, by and large, the unsavoury side of our
environment that's to blame, such as smoky chimneys,
polluted air, and chemical additives to food. These things
are regularly investigated and, by and large, are found
fairly guiltless. What's to blame is probably our way of life
itself, such as eating meat, eating fat, drinking, not taking
exercise, and so forth. It's still necessary to say 'probably'
because the exact causal relationships haven't yet been
worked out; but if privileged man suffers more cancers
than unprivileged man – which is certainly the case – it is
axiomatic that those privileges are suspect and should be
examined.

What is so interesting is to wonder whether we will do
anything about them as soon as the causal relationships
have been worked out. Will we give up fat or bacon or sugar
or butter if they are found to be guilty? Will the Japanese
give up their tacky kind of rice if this is found to relate to
their phenomenal incidence of stomach cancer? Or will we
all disregard the findings, carefully worked out by
scientific statisticians, and carry on as before? If the
cigarette smokers are anything to go by, we will carry on

as before. We'll dismiss the warnings, and go on doing the things we like doing: over-eating, over-drinking, not walking much, driving a lot – and smoking. It has been calculated that the Americans now smoking are denying themselves a total of 267 million years of life. And yet they go on smoking. As a species we're unbelievably adamant in the face of the facts.

If we really want to be afflicted by cancer less in the immediate future, in the 50 (at least) years before science comes up with an answer, the only possible thing we can do is prevent ourselves from doing the things thought most likely to lead to cancer. Therefore, instead of spending £25 million on cancer research, which is the current figure, we ought to divert that money into prevention. With that kind of advertising budget, we could be certain of cutting down on smoking, and lung cancer would then be toppled from its Number One position in the cancer league. Prevention would be a short-term benefit, instead of the long-term solution that science is looking for, but it would be beneficial now in terms of lives saved for this generation.

Anyway, the chances are, when we do know the causes of the common cancers, that we'll look the other way, and wish that science will come up with an answer so that we can do what we like *and* not get cancer. The smokers are already showing the way, disregarding the facts, carrying on with their pleasure, and suffering in consequence. And I expect the rest of us will be no different when other cancer causes come to light. We'll disregard the facts, and carry on as usual.

In short, as Haldane said, 'cancer's a funny thing'. We loathe it, we fear it, and we spend millions on it; but, if the smokers are no different from the rest of us, we won't let it change our lives. We'll look at the facts, and then look the other way. So, if cancer's a funny thing, we're a darn sight funnier.

Bicycles

Bicycles have been in my mind of late, partly because I went into a shop to buy one. I appreciate that many of us have been thinking in the same direction recently, remembering the excellent qualities of this invention, of its low energy input per passenger-mile, and its even lower output of fumes, noise or other noxious by-product. There is nothing quite like a bicyle, for economy, for lack of insult to the environment, for getting swiftly from A to B, or C or D. I calculated that, even if I purchased a new bicycle, the capital outlay would have been repaid by the time I had saved myself 100 return journeys on the London Underground. In three months of going to work the admirable bicyle would have earned its keep, and thereafter it would be downhill all the way. So, I walked into the bicycle shop and, reasonably enough, there were rows and rows of bicyles. They were all new, and I remembered again all those childhood hours with cotter-pins and hub brakes, with intestinal tubes and bubbles in the water bucket, French chalk and eternal joy. But I suddenly remembered the awful crash. How many of us were involved, and were we all full-grown men at the time as we thundered into each other to fill the road with bodies and bikes from one ditch right to the other. What a smash-up that had been! And quite a while ago.

The Royal Air Force that I knew went in for a policy of dispersal. This meant that everything was a long way from everything else. The sleeping huts were a mile from the ablutions, and these were at a distance from the mess and, as for the airfield itself, that was at least a couple of miles away from any bed, shower, or porridge-ful tureen. In order that we, the airmen, should triumph over these various distances, and actually reach work before it was time to head back for the next meal, we were each issued with a bicycle. At least, that was the theory and, when I arrived just after the war at my first dispersed airfield, it seemed to work in practice as the place was alive with 1,500 bicycles of every colour and kind. Confidently, therefore, I went into the bicycle shed to be suitably equipped.

'Sign here,' said the man behind the counter.

I signed, and looked up to see my bicycle. Red was a colour that I had fancied, and red it was. Unfortunately, what it wasn't worried me more at the time. It wasn't with wheels, or handlebars, or a saddle, let alone such refinements as pedals or a chain. In fact, as I saw it, it wasn't even a bike.

'That's not a bike,' I said.

'It's the best we've got,' he said. 'You've just got to build on that frame, and would you mind carrying it out of here as I'm shutting up.'

So I carried out the frame, and set off on the four miles back to my hut.

'New here?' said the first airman who pedalled by.

'Yes,' I said.

'New here?' said the second airman who pedalled by.

And then there was a third airman, and a fourth, and I suppose about 1,500 before I reached the hut. There I threw down that frame, and threw down my own bulk on the allotted bed, before asking those with bikes, with full bikes, how they had achieved such a plethora of extras, such as wheels, chains and handlebars.

The system, I learned, was to take the needed parts from some airman who had been posted somewhere else. He had to hand in some sort of bike but, just as the bike-shed wasn't too fussy about the kind of bike it issued, it also didn't trouble too much about the bikes it received from those who were departing.

'As soon as you hear of someone who's going,' said a man three beds away from mine, 'you want to nip round smartish, and take anything that he's got spare.'

Later that very evening I did hear of someone who was going, and nipped round on my own two feet, only to arrive like the last vulture at a kill. The man's bicycle had been stripped of all but its frame, and that he was hanging on to, but that I already had. Plainly, as any right-thinking vulture realises, it is necessary to be quicker off the mark.

It is no good arriving when the thing is the bicycular
equivalent of skin and bones.

There was plenty of incentive to do so. Having no bike
meant getting last to the cookhouse, and last to work, and
last back home again, all of which were disagreeable in
their differing fashions. I had to get myself something
more rideable than a frame; something, for example, with
wheels. I had already realised that not every machine
which hurtled past me was a bicycle in the total sense of
the word, and not every wheel, for instance, had rubber
round its rim. These travesties of bikes, noisy, skidding
and occasionally despatching sparks from the road
surface, would have induced tears in any manufacturer,
but they brought no tears to my eyes because, however
much they proceeded in fits and sparks, they definitely
proceeded, and faster than my two feet. As I belatedly
reached the mess, then work, and then the mess again
each lunchtime, these bits of bikes were always ahead of
me, silently jeering at my late arrival. This was not good
enough.

After two weeks of considerable effort I had done
wonders, having achieved two wheels and a handlebar.
The lack of a saddle meant that it was necessary to ride,
jockey-like, with airborne buttocks while I used the frame
for a stirrup, and the lack of tyres meant that curves were
well nigh impossible, but I was excellent on the straight
and clattered along in fine style to arrive at each
destination, stone-deaf and weary, but at least ahead of
the pedestrians. Of course, I couldn't pedal, being without
pedals and chain; but what are such minutiae when the
wind is blowing through one's hair, the sparks are at one's
feet, and the road ahead is straight, empty and downhill.

A friend with pedals made me realise that this further
technological leap was still ahead of me. However, the
thought was not immediate because I could always travel
faster than he could, a success made easier by the fact that
he was short on handlebars. He was so short of them that
he had nothing but half a broomstick jammed into the
requisite hole in the frame. His pedalling was fine, but he
had great difficulty in getting sufficient twist on to that
upright handle. In fact his energetic and skilled pedalling

merely meant that each time he ran off the road he did so
very speedily. He too had no tyres but, in a hare-and-
tortoise fashion, we were evenly matched. The time he
took in getting out of each hedge was roughly the time I
took in walking up each hill.

'Wish I had one of your pedals,' I said to him one day.

'Wish I had a handlebar,' he replied, and soon the deal
was done.

We sawed my handlebars in half – they are, after all,
called a pair of handlebars – and he had one of them and I
had the other. We then amputated one of his pedals, and
grafted it onto my machine. There was a certain amount of
discussion as to whether the pedal should be on the same
side as the single handlebar, and we each opted for no very
sound reason to have them on opposing sides. I had a left
pedal and a right bar, he therefore a left bar and a right
pedal, and in tandem – so to speak – we set off to try the
new arrangement. After but a hedge or two it worked
wonderfully well, and better still once we had tied our
pedalling feet to their pedals, in order to be able to lift them
up as well as push them down. Our other legs hung
uselessly, and any attempt to pedal as well with them
through the frame led instantly to another hedge. We did
try leaning against each other, much perhaps as horses do
in the traces, but this too – although it regularised the
number of pedals and handlebars – was better in theory
than practice. Or perhaps more practice would have done
the trick. It certainly would all have been easier with a
saddle while he – my other half so to speak – preferred to sit
across the cross-bar and pedal and steer from there.

Thus equipped, and almost as fast as all our fellows, and
much faster on occasion as some of them had brakes, the
ambition to better our machines was less urgent than it
had been formerly. Tyres would have been nice, and would
certainly have got us quicker off the mark. Without them it
is possible to pedal for quite a while, with the back wheel
revolving merrily, before the bike actually appreciates
what you have in mind and bothers to move forward. But
that was such a detail compared with the pre-requisite of
having wheels. Much to our surprise and although a
proper bicycle seems pared to the bone of unnecessary

extras it was possible to dispense with almost everything
when need be, and that airfield was racked with need.
Hardly anyone had a bicycle truly worthy of the name.
What they had as substitute was mobile bits of bike.

Then came the day of the dreadful crash. It happened
just before lunch and was made worse by our entire
squadron of planes choosing that time to land. We couldn't
cross the main runway when they were using it, and about
a thousand of us accumulated waiting for a green light.
This given we then set off like the biggest grand prix of
them all, every man determined not to be thousandth in
line at the mess which was our destination. The ones
without tyres did all that pedalling before their bikes
began to move. Those short on pedals pulled frantically
with the lengths of string that, if tugged and released
alternately, and properly attached, would do the job that
pedals normally do. And those with half a handlebar put
both hands on that single half, the better to control the
front-wheel wobble that comes with speed.

I do not know how the accident began, but I know it
occurred at the bottom of the slope. I had a momentary
vision of one jockey, with buttocks held high above the spike
of steel where his saddle should have been, and I know he
was out of control. A cross-bar passenger tried to fend him
off and did so too effectively, sending himself backwards
and the jockey too far forwards. Thereafter it was nothing
but sparks, hideous noise, metal upon tarmac, and metal
upon metal with people in between. The brakeless ones
had no choice, save to select an area in front of them full of
bodies more than bikes, and into this they crashed without
a drop in speed. I saw one man almost climb up his handle-
broom, the better to escape the carnage down below; but, of
course, it got him in the end. He landed on the scores and
scores of men already there.

Suddenly there was a shout of quite a different order
above all the yells of pain. 'Petrol,' it said, and so there
was, great fumes of it from a hundred broken bottles
wrapped up in haversacks. We all scattered like rabbits,
fearful of a fire. But the stolen aviation spirit just vanished
into earth and air and let us be. Those with motorbikes
bemoaned this loss, as it had been vital, for weekends, for

long-distance girl-friends, for barter with civilians. And
we all knew that petrol was streets ahead of bicycles,
better than pedal power any day, the fuel we longed for as
soon as each of us had some machine into which to pour
the stuff. The day of bicycles was past. Even if they had
tyres, saddles, brakes, mudguards, chains, pedals and
handlebars, they were not for us. We had seen enough of
them, along with uniforms, billets and all the rest.
Motorbikes were what we wanted, and cars best of all.

As I stood in the shop the other day, dazzled by all those
bikes, all spanking new, and all with 3-speeds, 5-speeds,
10-speeds, and lights, and horns, tool-bags, locks, pumps,
they became as spots before my eyes. It didn't seem right
that there should be so many of them, all so very new.
Where was the struggle, save in finding the cash? Where
was the joy of assembly, week by week, as other parts
came to light? And where was the skill in riding
something that had everything a rider could need?

'Don't you have any that are second hand?' I said to the
youth in charge.

'No call for them,' he said.

So I left, on two feet and not two wheels. It didn't seem
right just buying one. I thought of explaining to the young
man. But I didn't. So, I've taken the liberty of explaining to
you instead how it's very hard, for some of us, just to go
and buy a bike.

Puberty

I heard a man complain the other day that he never had been a teenager; and he had a point. Once upon a time schoolboys were suddenly transformed into adults without the interregnum that is today identified with the term 'teenager'. There wasn't the raucous, independent, moderately wealthy period, bridging the gap between normal childhood and normal adulthood. I don't know when the term 'teenager' was first used, and have tried to find out, but it surely didn't come into being, as I see it, until sexual awakening got in on the act, and that has been a matter of changing biology rather than changing social custom.

At the beginning of the nineteenth century it was highly improbable that anyone still in her teens in Britain would, for example, be having children. The average age of menarche, or first menstruation, was then about 17½. As the ability to conceive tends to arrive a year or two after menarche, and as any conception takes its three-quarters of a year before being born, it was then highly likely that a girl was out of her teens before she gave birth, irrespective of anything that society itself might be saying about a good age for marriage or a proper time for intercourse.

With boys it is much harder to be definite about the onset of fertility in a previous century, partly because there is no convenient yardstick like menarche. But everyone is agreed that sexual development occurred much later then than it does today, and was probably as relatively late with boys as it was with girls. Certainly the fragments of evidence that do exist all point in the same direction. For example, of the choirboys who were in Bach's choir in Leipzig in the eighteenth century, the altos were, on average, 4.7 years older than they are today.

At the start of the last century, as I have said, menarche happened at age 17½. By 1880 it happened at 16. By 1920 it was less than 15, and today it happens, on average, just over the age of 13. But while this has been going on all sorts of other events, related to the time of maturity, have been moving in a contrary direction. For example, in England, girls could marry at the age of 12 and boys at the age of 14 until 1929, provided they had parental consent to do so. In 1929, despite the substantial reduction by then in the age of sexual maturity, the minimum marriage age was raised to 16 for both sexes. The young couple still had to get parental consent – up to the age of 21, hence all the visits to Gretna Green because Scottish law was more lenient. The age of majority was lowered from 21 to 18 in 1969, but this still means that no one can be married here until 16, which is substantially older than it was half a century ago, even though the age of sexual maturity has been coming down all the time.

Other countries reflect this confusion over when a girl is no longer a child but a woman. In Spain girls can marry at 12. In Italy, a similarly Catholic country, they cannot do so until they are 18. In Hungary they can marry at 14, but in East Germany, Poland and Yugoslavia, they can't until 18. For Belgium and France the minimum is 15, but for Sweden and Switzerland it is 18. The United Kingdom is, therefore – at 16 – in the middle, but with that proviso about consent bringing the age up to 18. The United States is similarly confused, with the law varying from state to state. California, for example, doesn't permit girls to marry until they are 18 but allows them access to free contraceptives from the age of 12.

In other words, with marriages being permitted either as early as 12 or as late as 18, the law-makers don't seem to be paying too much attention to the actual age of sexual development, or to the fact that this has come down so substantially in recent decades. Of course, sexual development doesn't necessarily mean that the people concerned are either ready for marriage or want marriage; but it does relate to their sexual activity. And longings. And behaviour. A biological law would permit marriage, say, a couple of years after menarche, which would today make the age 15 for the average girl. Boys tend to be fertile somewhat earlier, but society in this country doesn't seem to be ready yet for such early marriages, or rather for putting the clock back to the time when such marriages

were permitted. One reason, which has apparently been
going against the fact of earlier development, is education.

In the old days, or rather when schooling became
available for all in 1870, the requirement was that children
should attend school from the age of 5 to the age of 10.
Gradually this leaving age has been raised, and it stands
now at 16. In other words, when universal education was
started, it was virtually impossible for a schoolgirl to
become pregnant. Since then, with menarche coming
down by more than three years and with the school-
leaving age going up by six years, the two lines on the
graph have crossed, and it is now very possible for a
schoolgirl to become pregnant. In the past menarche
happened, on average, over seven years *after* a girl left
school. It is now happening, on average, almost three
years *before* she leaves school. With boys, although less
well documented, the story is very similar. In the past they
left school before reaching sexual maturity, and today it
happens while they're still at school.

Once again the differing laws in different countries
reflect not just religious attitudes, but society's confusion.
It is obviously good that children are receiving better food,
and therefore maturing earlier. It is obviously good that
they are attending school for a longer period. But the fact
that school*girls* can now become, so to speak, school*women*,
and be sexually potent as well as active, has created a
situation which some countries still choose to deny.
Whereas Sweden, for example, actually requires sex
education in schools, and certainly permits information
on contraception to be part of that education, lots of other
countries deny that kind of teaching to their pubescent
pupils. Spain, for instance, actively prohibits information
on contraception, and will only tolerate sex education in
schools if all talk of contraception is omitted. Coming
nearer to home, Ireland is the same, prohibiting sex
education if contraception is included in it. As someone
said, there has never been any need to teach the human
race how to copulate, and sex education therefore means
contraception education. Or as Lord Byron put it, in an
anguished and conclusive little rhyme:

Oh Mary Mother, I believe,
thou did'st not sin but did conceive.
Mary Mother, still believing,
teach me to sin without conceiving.

In Britain it would seem as if quite a few youngsters are
still short of the information that Byron was longing for;
or, if they do possess it, have disregarded it, for every year
there are almost 5,000 pregnancies among schoolgirls who
have not yet reached their sixteenth birthday. The figures
generally start with the 11-year-olds, and then increase
each year to reach a maximum with the 15-year-olds.
Perhaps contraceptive teaching, when and where it
happens, should start rather earlier than it does. Leaving
it until age 13 or thereabouts is leaving it too late for many
girls as menarche now starts, on average, at 13, which
means that half are menstruating before that time.

Certainly the official figures don't give much cause for
complacency about pre-16 pregnancies. In 1951 there were
193 births in this country to girls under 16. By 1956 that
figure had risen to 260, by 1961 to 870, by 1966 to 1,270, and
by 1976 to 1,420. That's a sevenfold leap in 25 years. The
number of schoolgirl abortions has also been going up.
The act permitting legal abortions was only introduced in
1968, but in the following complete year there were 1,200
legal abortions to the under-16s. By 1972 there were 3,200
and by 1975 almost 3,400. Hence the forlorn cry in a
British Medical Journal leading article that 'some 5,000
British girls a year are becoming pregnant before they
have much idea what life has to offer'. It also means that
5,000 homes a year are hit by this particular form of
mishap, as one girl in every 400 proves that her biological
maturity is well in advance of that generally acceptable to
the society in which she lives.

What now of the boys – if that is the right word – who are
making all these girls pregnant? Well, in theory and
according to law, they are guilty. An offence has been
committed, but the girl can never be at fault. However
much she may have enticed her lover she is the victim of
the offence. He is also guiltless if under the age of 14. But, if
he is older, and the girl is less than 16, there is a maximum

gaol sentence of two years. If the girl is under 13 there is a possible life imprisonment for the male in question. However, it is easy to suspect that the law, which is plainly behind the times, will change before too long. A recent survey discovered that 31 per cent of boys and 13 per cent of girls had had their first sexual experience before they were 16.

There seems to me one obvious line of thought. If better nutrition and better everything is making us mature younger, then our ages do not correspond to the ages of our forebears. The 13-year-old girl of today, however much she may be at school, is the 16-year-old of the last century who had already been working for some years. Similarly, the 4-year-old of today is the 5-year-old of the last century. So why don't we slip everything earlier? Go to school at 4, not 5? Do our O-levels one year earlier? Leave school one year earlier? Be allowed to marry one year earlier? And begin to recognise the fact that, biologically, we are not as we used to be even a century ago, and when they first sent us to school, aged five?

Rabies

So far as I can remember there have only been two things that have really frightened my daughter Laura. The first was the music for *Doctor Who*. She would watch the programmes well enough, but run out of the room at that music. However, the second frightening event is the one that I wish to dwell on, namely the first time she spotted a rabies poster at one of the Channel ports. It said 'Rabies Brings Death' and there was a picture of a skull to hit home the message yet more forcefully. Laura, not very old at the time, was soon in floods of tears, and of course that was distressing, but I am wondering about the actual message, that 'Rabies Brings Death'. After all, the strident tone, the awful warning, the skull, would seem to imply that, above all else, we should fear rabies, as if it were the plague about to arrive on our shores and destroy, say, a quarter of the people living here.

These doubts can hit us all when we travel to the continent of Europe where rabies does thrive. Currently it exists from eastern France right across most of eastern Europe north of the Alps. So, when we're having a picnic near Strasbourg, or Frankfurt, or Munich, we're in the heart of rabies country. And, of course, it's all very peaceful, and we meet people and dogs and see foxes and it's exactly like home. It isn't full of slobbering creatures, foaming with saliva, crazed with fear at the very sight of water. In fact, it looks much as Britain would look if rabies managed to leap across the Channel, and make itself endemic here. So, at this point, we think again about these posters, and wonder if they're not crying 'wolf' at us, and whether the Government shouldn't be warning us about some real dangers, like nuclear war or step-ladders.

So how dangerous is rabies to people as, presumably, it is people that we're most concerned about? Well, let's take Europe first, where the disease has been rife ever since the end of the last war. In the last quarter of last year there were four cases of rabies among humans throughout the continent. As that's among 400 million people it means that we, if similarly attacked, could expect one, or perhaps two, cases a year. In the United States, where the disease has always been endemic, they are having a bit of an epidemic right now with four deaths or so a year. They are calling it an epidemic because this is twice the average for the previous 10 years. In 1977, for example, there was one case. Naturally it is sad whenever anybody dies before his time, but the numbers of deaths do have to be seen in comparison with other kinds of death, and I'm sure more people die from slipping on hamburgers in the United States than from rabies. In Europe lightning is a bigger killer than is rabies, and over in the United States, where natural calamities are much more a way of life than here, practically anything you can think of, such as tornadoes, volcanoes, hail, snow, rain, flood, falling trees, landslides – they each kill far more on average than rabies has done.

I mentioned step-ladders just now because they are a major cause of death. So, the other day, when I was reading a novel about someone bringing a dog back here across the Channel, and how this innocent little thing was loved and then the death of all concerned, I began to replace the word 'dog', wherever it occurred with 'step-ladder', and the novel improved at once. 'Little did she think, as they loaded the step-ladder on board, that they were loading death ... "I hear you've a step-ladder," said the village constable, looking anxiously at the young couple.' And so he should have done, if he wanted to keep death down in his district. He should also have had a look at their electrical fittings, their loose tiles, their stair-rods, their cooked and unrefrigerated meat, their slippery bath-room tiles; potential killers every one. As for their dog, well he'd worry about that if he had time.

It's also pertinent to remember that we used to have rabies in this country, and until fairly recently. For example, many of the deer in Richmond Park succumbed to it towards the end of the last century. The last British human to die of it, having contracted the disease from an animal within Britain, did so in 1902, and the disease itself died out here round about that time. There was a further brief flurry after World War One, brought about – it is thought – by a dog brought back on a troopship, but no more cases were reported after 1922. Ten years ago there were the so-called Camberley and Newmarket outbreaks when two dogs in quite separate incidents, and after their six-months' quarantine, developed rabies. At Camberley there followed a Governmental slaughtering of wildlife in the area, now generally considered to have been an ill-planned reaction, and the outbreaks are widely presumed to have resulted from faulty quarantine rather than anything more insidious. At all events there was rabies again in this country for a brief spell, but it didn't spread. We are still, in short, rabies-free.

But we do, as with the death posters and with considerable publicity given to everything remotely connected with the disease, make a great song and dance about rabies. It is a Number One terror word, and actively maintained in a Number One slot. We spend about £1 million a year in keeping ourselves rabies-free, and emotionally would spend ten times that figure, or so one suspects, if this was thought necessary. But as threats go to human life it is, as I have indicated from endemic Europe, a fairly minor issue. Even the vets make the same sort of point when contemplating other zoonoses, those diseases transmitted from animals to man. To quote from a special issue on Rabies in the *Veterinary Record*: 'When all is taken into account it is worthwhile recalling that the risks of rabies to the human community of this country have been considerably over-emphasised in relation to the hazards related to already prevalent zoonoses, like toxocariasis, toxoplasmosis and leptospiral jaundice, of which the general public remains happily unaware'. Well, toxocariasis, for example, is the very nasty disease that's been getting some publicity of late because people can get it from dogs, via canine excrement, and it does cause fatalities although blindness is more frequent. But how many of us can even spell that disease's name, let alone fear it as we view some of the 500 tons of faeces dropped by British dogs each day.

Now that dogs have, so to speak, wormed their way into the argument it's interesting to reflect upon the part they play in our loathing of rabies. The conventional picture is of a mad dog, whether a previous pet or a freelance hound, going insanely berserk, biting all who come within range, and distributing death wholesale. But, in Europe, dogs only form a small proportion of the numbers of animals which get rabies every year. For example, among the domesticated animals, about as many cows have been getting it. Sheep and horses are about two-thirds of the dog total. But, moving to the wild, far and away the greatest victim in Europe is the fox. Even though a lot of foxes must die unknown deaths, and few dogs do, the number of known fox fatalities is about 10 times the dog level. Among other wild animals the badger suffers, so too the mustelids such as the stoats and weasels, and so too the deer. The reason, I suspect, we so strongly associate dogs with rabies is not so much because of our affection for dogs but because dogs are the principal vectors of the disease for man. Hardly any humans do get the disease in Europe, as I've already indicated, but those very few that do so tend to get it from a dog.

The other known fact about rabies, as etched into our consciousness as the formula Rabies=dog=death, is the absolute conviction that it is highly infectious and will spread like wildfire once it gets a grip. Well, it has had quite a good grip on Europe in the three post-war decades, and has been spreading from its alleged starting place in Poland. The rate of spread has been about 18 miles a year, but this slows down when it reaches some obstacle. When the advance reached the Rhine it was halted for seven years, despite the fact that there are bridges, tunnels, boats going from bank to bank, and people taking their pets back and forth every day. The disease is now in France, but making laggardly progress. Occasionally a dead animal is found a hundred miles or so ahead of the advance, like a soldier too far in front of his fellows, but these isolated cases don't infect the neighbourhood, any more than the soldier's brave advance affects the actual front line. So, it still doesn't stand, like some Napoleon, on the French coast with nothing but the Channel keeping it at bay. If the barrier of the Rhine is anything to go by, the barrier of the Channel will be quite formidable even if nothing is done to counter the rabid invasion of our shores.

In short, rabies doesn't seem to be particularly, well, rabid. The dictionary defines that word as 'furious, violent' and yet its progress towards us has been almost leisurely. It has nothing of the virulence of, for example, myxomatosis which felled the rabbit population in a matter of months. Or of, say, a new strain of influenza which can get hundreds of thousands of us by the throat in an even shorter time, and kill quite a few of us into the bargain, such as that epidemic of 1919 which killed as many as the war had done. We would do better, I suspect, to turn back every foreigner with a runny nose at our ports rather than let him in and only jump on him, and fine him (up to £400), and gaol him (if need be), should he happen to have a dog about his person. Most of those caught and found guilty are foreign citizens who travel here with their pets just as they do in the rest of Europe.

So, what would happen if we dropped the ban, let people bring in pets, saved the expense of £1 million a year in prevention, and watched to see for how much longer the Channel could keep out rabies than the Rhine was able to do? Despite its laggardliness, I suppose it would get here in time. And probably via a dog or a cat.

Well, once we had rabies what would be the drawbacks and the expense. The drawbacks - if that's the right word - are that a lot of our wild animals would die, foxes in particular and so would some of our domestic animals, notably dogs, cats and cows, and so would a very few of us. Two Frenchmen, for example, have so far died from it this century. The expense of having rabies in Britain would be much greater than the cost of keeping it out, mainly because of all the vaccination that would be involved, of our millions of dogs, cats, and cattle. And that, so say all concerned, is a very considerable reason for keeping rabies out. But it doesn't look so well on the posters, does it? Instead of 'Rabies Kills' there would be 'Rabies Costs'. It may be a greater and more important truth, but it doesn't deter so well. Or might we all react one day against those posters, and consider they have cried, not just 'Wolf' but 'Rabid Wolf', too long and much too loudly?

The Smith Family

On 14 September a Boeing 747 will take off from Kingsford Smith Airport, Sydney, and Captain Smith will be given permission to do so by Flight Controller Smith in the Kingsford Smith control tower. First Officer Smith will help him in the take-off procedure, and so will Flight Engineer Smith. In the cabin section chief steward Smith and the other cabin staff, every one a Smith, will cater for the needs of all the passengers, every single one of them also a Smith. The flight, principally organised by Dick Smith, a wealthy electronics executive, is scheduled to last two hours, and will fly over or near some 200 places in Australia with Smith in their names, such as Smith's waterhole which is way out back of Birdsville. The trip will also fly over or near the homes of some 30,000 Smiths, and every ticket for the flight will have been completed by Barry Smith of Howard Smith Travel. On board, Smith's Crisps will be eaten, washed down by wine from the Smith's vineyards. No one will be allowed to join the flight unless he or she is a Smith, but exceptions will be made for those who wish to change their name to Smith by deed poll during the flight. And, of course, there will be prizes for the youngest Smith on board, the oldest one, the most Smiths from one family, the most from one company, the greatest number with the same Christian name, and on and on. For Smiths, at least, it will be the flight of the century. And it's all for charity.

The charity that the flight is supporting is called, somewhat reasonably at this stage in the story, The Smith Family. And the reason I am mentioning this particular organisation is not because of some patronymic adulation for the name but because, in my opinion, it is the very best charity that I have ever encountered. The flight of the 747 just happens to be a publicity performance organised on its behalf. And good luck to it, as it hopes to raise 20,000

Australian dollars. However, my main interest is in the charity itself.

It was founded in Australia in 1922 by five men who put on a party that Christmas for a group of deprived kids. When asked afterwards by the Matron of that children's institution who should be thanked, the men said 'Just thank Mr Smith'. Not one of them had that name, but that was their way of remaining anonymous, and this spur-of-the-moment answer provided the title for the organisation they then created. They appreciated that poor people are not just poor at Christmas-time, and they set up The Smith Family as their way of providing a permanent welfare organisation. Its president today is called Mr Smith, whatever his actual name may be, and the organisation over which he presides is the largest private welfare business in Australia. It is most active in New South Wales, but has also moved into Canberra and Victoria, and has every intention of spreading right across the country. It gives away about £6 million of charity every year, mainly as clothing, but it wasn't the size of this sum that impressed me. Instead it was the manner of its giving, and also the manner of its receiving.

Let's deal with the giving first. And let's deal with that by describing some apocryphal person arriving at The Smith Family's headquarters in Sydney. Let's assume a woman arrives on her own in a Pontiac. It's not the newest of Pontiacs, but it's a large American car all the same, and she parks it just outside the main entrance. She certainly doesn't park it round the corner just for the sake of keeping the thing out of sight. Anyway, in she goes, and there she looks for the clothing counter to tell of her needs. At home, she explains, there are three children in need of clothes, and she herself could do with a sweater or two to help her through the forthcoming winter.

The first question from the Smith Family assistant is *not* some form of mini-means test, about *why* she needs these clothes, or *how* her family got in such a state that she must beg for clothes. Instead it's about size, and how big the children are so that they can be kitted out correctly.

'Well, Johnny's 4, and Bruce is 6, and Linda is 9, but she's tall for her age, and doesn't like bright colours.'

So assistant and visitor walk down the lines, selecting as need be, and eventually the visitor leaves, laden down with garments and extremely grateful for all the help. The Smith Family's policy on such visitors is absolutely straightforward and, in my opinion, quite admirable. If someone actually comes and asks for second-hand clothes, then they need clothes. It's as simple as that. There isn't any talk whatsoever about her turning up in a Pontiac. Why should there be? Australia being the size it is, and her home almost certainly quite a way from The Smith Family, she's almost bound to come in a car, however short she is of money, however short of clothes.

So the *giving* policy is primarily to give, and with as little fuss as possible. The *receiving* policy, which I found equally impressive, is equally straightforward, partly because it is so businesslike. The principal receiving business of The Smith Family is to collect old clothes. Most important of all, it will happily do the collecting. In certain parts of Sydney it will collect every day, and all you have to do is to call them. In more outlying districts it will only collect a couple of times a week. To encourage you to give clothes they deliver bags to houses, and come round to collect them, whether full or empty, on the following day. In other words, they don't expect you to do all the work, to have the original idea of cleaning out your cupboards, to get your clothes to a centre in town, to do what can so easily be put off to another day. They do the lion's share of what is necessary to get old clothes from you.

They then do all the sorting, firstly into clothes still fit to wear and those which are not. The fit-to-wear go on to the appropriate pegs and are given away, as to the lady in the Pontiac. Those unfit to wear are then sorted into their various categories. For example, the woollens are sold to be mixed with new wool to make carpets, blankets and so on. Cottons are cut into handkerchief-sized pieces, and are then sold to the engineering industry as wiper cloths. The Australian Navy, for example, gets all its wiper cloths from The Smith Family. Needless to say, all buttons and zips have to be removed before anything can be sold as a cloth, but the advantage of all this selling is that it earns sufficient revenue to cover every overhead of the business itself, all the salaries, the collecting vans, the warehousing. So, if any actual money is given to The Smith Family, exactly 100 per cent of this money can be given to the needy. Some of our very best charities in this country consume 80 per cent of the money they receive and, therefore, have only 20 per cent to give away. Hardly any are able to give away 100 per cent of their donations.

So, to sum up thus far, The Smith Family collects good clothes and gives them away. It collects unuseable clothes and turns them into money. And it collects money and gives it all away.

As smaller sidelines it also collects furniture and tins of food. Once again the prevailing attitude is that a lot of people have a lot of objects at home which they no longer want, and which aren't at all valuable in the ordinary sense of that word, such as old clothes, old and unimportant furniture (like beds), and tins of food. People, so say The Smith Family, are much more willing to give away *things*, particularly things they no longer want, than they are willing to give away money which, in a sense and whoever they are, they always want. Anyway, as with the clothes, the furniture is divided into useable, which means it can be given away, or unuseable in which case it's repaired as much as possible and then sold at a store called The White Elephant. The tins of food are first sorted, and then made into hampers to be given away to the needy. If the sorting wasn't done first, then someone might receive nothing but tins and tins of anchovies which, however needy the recipient, is not the kind of gift that's needed.

What I like about all this, this collection of old clothes, furniture and food, is that I bet 90 per cent of our British homes contain a very great deal of unwanted clothes, furniture and even food. What about those old tins in the cupboard that you once bought but no one likes and you feel reluctant just to throw away? What about that old bed that you would really throw away if you knew where to throw it? As for clothes, they shrink, they fade, they lose their elbows, they get out of fashion, or you just don't like them any more. What about them? It doesn't seem right just throwing them into the dustbin. Admittedly, they could go to a local jumble sale, and there be picked up for 10p or so, but the jumble expects you to do the work, to have the clear-out, to take your offerings to the village hall, to have them picked over by some toffee-nosed neighbour, and to see them sold for some pittance to yet another neighbour who may or may not be deserving. I still have, for example, my demobilisation suit. I never liked it. I've never worn it. I'm not certain anyone else would like to wear it, but I certainly don't wish to put it in the rubbish bin. Our waste business must be the most wasteful business of them all, burying as it does so many of the once-used products of our consumer age, and I see no point in my suit being used to help fill a swamp somewhere by the Hackney Marshes. In time moth or even rust may get at it, and then I'll be too ashamed of the thing for it to be sneered at in a jumble or sent on its way to Bangladesh.

In short, I like The Smith Family and wish we had it here. I like the ease with which it gives away, and I like the easy way that it receives. I like that 100 per cent of the money sent to it is then sent on to someone else, and so I wish Captain Smith well on his charity flight with his load of 400 Smiths as he takes off from Kingsford Smith and heads for 22 Smith's Creeks, and Smith's River, Smith's Bluff, Mount Smith, Smith's Gully, Smith's Shed, Smith's Swamp, Smith's Bore, Smith's Pool, Smith's Pinnacle, and so many other Smith spots that one imagines every man jack of every vessel taking British citizens to that continent must have been a Smith to have named this new land so single-mindedly. Not every one of those early voyagers must have considered that charity began at home. But every one called Smith could take extra pride in the fact that such an excellent and brand-new charity bearing their name was created in this brand-new land.

Dogs

Once upon a time, as we all know, these British Isles possessed some large beasts. There were, for example, the wolf and the bear. In those days of old, knights had to be reasonably bold, I suppose, just to ride about in the countryside when, at any moment, a bear could emerge and care nothing for all their gay caparisons. Thank goodness, we all say, that a walk in the country today might bring us face to face with a harvest mouse but will certainly not be the death of us. Such large wild animals as there are will scurry away at the very sound of us, and we will be fortunate if we even catch a glimpse of them.

So what must it be like in those countries which have animals that do occasionally attack the local residents? Well, to help answer this question, and give some idea of the situation, I'd like to describe a country I know quite well which is ravaged by a particular animal. I don't want to name the animal just yet because, if I do, then all your preconceived notions about that animal will immediately become involved. For the same sort of reason I won't mention the country either, as you will then start picturing to yourself what you know of that land. Instead I'd just like to give you some of the facts and let them speak for themselves.

Well, the animal in question isn't always vicious. Mostly it's fairly docile, but there are millions of them and so the antagonistic members of this species do add up to a considerable total. All in all, despite – as I have said – it being a peaceable animal, it makes about 240,000 attacks on humans every year. The country's population is neither particularly large nor particularly small, and therefore the attack rate means that every inhabitant of the country stands about a one in 200 chance of being attacked each year. Average length of life for the ordinary citizen is about that for many western countries, and so this means that each individual stands roughly a 1 in 3 chance of

being attacked during his or her lifetime. Well, that's a lot
of attacks, and we here in Britain can shiver slightly at the
thought of such animal intransigence.

So, what, one might ask, are the authorities of that
country doing about all this violence? Needless to say,
there is concern, and the leading animal organisation
there has produced a helpful little pamphlet advising
locals what best to do should they encounter one of these
creatures when it is being, as the pamphlet euphemisti-
cally puts it, 'unfriendly'. There are, it says, seven rules.
First, never stare at the animal as this can be taken as a
threat. Second, do not show fear. The animal, it says, can
read fear in your eyes and body movements. So keep calm,
whistle, or walk slowly. Third, never run away from the
animal, as this may release its chase response and you
may be bitten as a result. So, always walk away slowly,
even backwards if need be to face the animal. Fourthly you
must observe how the animal is reacting to you. If it stays
put, or even backs away, it is probably recognising you as
dominant. But you must always be on your guard, and if it
shows its teeth you must realise that the time has come for
you to move away, slowly and backwards. Point 5:
remember that the animals have a territory to defend, and
this is an entirely natural act for them. Six: having meat in
your pocket is not always a good idea. And seven: most
people are attacked as they are retreating, so backing
away slowly is the most golden rule of all.

Heaven forbid, I can hear you all muttering, that we
should have an animal of that kind in our fair land. Let us
stick with the harvest mouse, and with the very occasional
glimpse of an otter, a badger or a roe deer as these animals
scurry away giving us no need to back, ever so cautiously,
away from them. So, isn't, you may ask, isn't the country
in question doing anything about these animals beyond
the issuing of pamphlets and trying to be helpful? It is, to
some extent. It tries to capture and kill those creatures
which have become particularly vindictive, and it kills
about 60,000 a year. That's quite a slaughter, but it still
doesn't take much of a bite out of the estimated population
of five million. It's some sort of compensation for the
farmers who estimate that they lose 6,000 domestic

animals a year as a result of attacks by the wild creatures, but many people argue that a slaughter rate of just 160 a day is nothing like enough. One can sympathise. The breeding rate of this species is more than capable of making good that loss from its basic population of five million.

Before I disclose which animal and which country I am talking about, I have before me a cutting from one of its newspapers. To me, this emphasises the bizarre reverence which the natives have for this animal, despite that appalling figure of 240,000 attacks every single year. The cutting refers to one particular attack, when a man's son was wounded to such an extent that 12 stitches were necessary. The man, which does seem reasonable, was incensed and went after the animal. He caught it, managed to put a length of cord around its neck, and strangled the creature which had so hideously harmed his son. The animal died, and the man buried it without more ado. So what happens? Is he commended for having destroyed an offensive animal with no cost to the State? Not at all. He is fined £50, ordered to pay £30 costs, and generally reprimanded by the court.

So, to sum up about this un-named animal in an un-named land: it makes 240,000 attacks on humans every year, it kills 6,000 livestock, it is officially put down at the rate of 60,000 individuals every year, the public are advised to stand still and back away if ever they are attacked or fear that they may be, and the creature itself - the cause of all this trouble - is so revered that a man is found guilty if he kills the creature that grieviously wounds his son.

OK, so I'll tell you where this is, and what it is, but please hold on to the opinion you have at the moment. I assume you have built up your own mental picture of the kind of creature I have been talking about, and the kind of land in which it operates - so don't let that picture go away, just because I tell you I am talking about the dog and I am talking about the United Kingdom. Don't now change mental gear just because Rover has never hurt a fly, and Fido couldn't if he tried. Remember that figure of 240,000 attacks each year, and how the man was got at by the

courts for killing the dog that mauled his son. How would
you feel if, say, a weasel or some berserk badger had
attacked your son? Or if somebody's pet monkey had leapt
over the garden wall and bitten so deeply that a dozen
stitches were necessary to bind the wound? My small son,
as it happened, was once bitten by a dog when in the park
one day, and the four canine punctures all drew blood. The
dog ran off, and the police didn't follow up the case
because my son had neither apprehended the dog nor felt
capable of giving a description beyond saying that it was
'fierce, big and unfriendly'. I wonder what would have
happened had he been bitten by a man? Or a pet ferret? Or
a rat? Or some animal just out from the local zoo?

It is thought, by the RSPCA and others, that there are
about half a million wild dogs in the country, the strays
that have no home. These are rounded up to some extent,
and about 60,000 are killed each year, but the scene isn't
quite what I once observed in a small Eskimo town in
northern Canada. The Eskimos didn't just kill a few of the
unwelcome strays; they killed the lot. We kill just a few:
60,000 a year out of the 500,000.

It is frequently said, notably by the politicians, that any
not-wholly-complimentary mention of dogs in this country will not so much have five million dogs at one's throat
as five million dog-owners. But it is interesting to note that
the tide seems to be turning, and the idea that dogs should
be controlled more effectively – that they should kill fewer
livestock, that they should bite fewer people, that they
should be less casual with the 500 tons of faeces they drop
every day, and their owners should actually pay towards
the trouble that they cause – all such ideas have been
gaining ground of late, and are not ridiculed as if dogs, like
Hindu cattle, should be above the law.

For example, there is an organisation called Jacopis.
However awkward the name, this body – the Joint
Advisory Committee on Pets in Society – has an
impeccable pedigree. It has an earl as its chairman, and is
supported by nine major national organisations, such as
the RSPCA. It wants dog wardens, about 600 or so, to help
control the dog population. After all, five million is a big
number, and one in 10 of us is a dog, so to speak, and 600

doesn't seem too big a number, considering the number of people who look after us. Well, who would pay for 600 wardens? At present the dog problem, and the rounding up and killing of strays, and the hospital bills, are all paid for by the State. Anyone who thinks that the dog licence covers some of this had better think again. In the good old days of 1796, when the licence was first established, the price was 3 to 5 shillings per dog, a sizeable hunk of money then. It became 12 shillings in 1854, but was dropped to 7s 6d in 1878, and there it has stayed ever since, except that we now call it 37½p. Really patriotic dog-owners should know that, as it costs about 60p for the State to collect each 37½p they are saving the State 22½p by not buying a dog licence. It is gratifying to learn, in these somewhat unpatriotic days, that about half Britain's dog-owners are sufficiently considerate in this fashion by forgetting to declare their possession of a dog.

Jacopis thinks the licence should start at £5 a year, which is the price of not many tins of Wolf-it-up, and this would pay for all those wardens, their dog-handling needs, and the cost of collecting the money in the first place. Even if it caused a drop in the dog population to, say, four million, that would still mean an income of £20 million a year. With that kind of budget the 600 wardens could actually do something about the half-million strays. And the thousands of car accidents caused every year by jay-walking dogs. And they might even clean up our city parks, and transform them from the turd world that they are often said to be.

We don't need another law for dogs. Let's just bring them into line with the rest of us, and make them pay via their owners for the trouble that they are. And let's all remember finally that case in Erith, Kent, last month. Two Dobermanns bit 11 people in 10 minutes, including 5 children, 1 policeman, and a 72-year-old woman. She, as it happened, died three days later. One of the dogs had already attacked a five-year-old boy and its owner had then been fined £10.

A Nun

It took me time to pluck up courage to ask her. I frequently saw her pedalling about the neighbourhood, propping her bike against the wall of the local school, leaning it outside tower blocks, and there were plenty of occasions for hailing her; but I was short on courage. What I wanted was to probe a bit, ask her how she made ends meet in these difficult days, what she lived on, and whether she received a fixed allowance from her community. In short, how does a nun get by?

So, I stopped the bike one day, summoned up a quite unnecesary amount of courage, and suggested we had lunch. 'I will have to ask,' she said, 'but I'll let you know.' In time she did let me know that the lunch could take place, and she could discuss with me just how much she received from her order, how it was spent, and whether she thought it was sufficient. She even welcomed the talk because economy was a subject dear to her heart. She liked not consuming more than was necessary, and didn't like waste, extravagance, and useless use of things. To put me in a suitable frame of mind for the meeting, I spent some of that morning listening on the radio to a trade unionist affirming that his members were receiving far short of a living wage, that their take-home pay was hardly sufficient to keep body and soul together, and that stark penury was their lot. With his words and figures still trembling in my ears I went off to lunch. I wanted to find out what one nun thought kept body and soul together.

To begin with – in our Indian restaurant – she explained that she belonged to an accredited lay order. This meant that she could work with the local parish and take lodgings in the area. She did not, in short, have to live in any kind of nunnery, but was independent, fending for herself, feeding herself, and living on her own. Her own community not only paid her upkeep but also sent the money to pay her rent. I was rather less interested in the

rent (which came to £71.60 a month, or £16.50 a week)
because there wasn't so much she could do about that. The
flat was, in a sense, inherited. It went with the job, was
expensive, but couldn't be altered. However, she could,
and did, make certain that the cost of living, of eating,
heating and getting about, was well below that figure for
the rent. In fact, she lived on less than £10 a week.

All that radio talk about a living wage, and body and
soul, boomed once again in my ears, and I asked her to
elaborate. I too, like the trade unionist, managed to
consume much more than that every week, even the most
spartan. I looked again at the black-and-white robed
woman sitting opposite, and wondered how she did it. She
neither looked famished, nor was she falling upon her
vegetable biriani and round poppadums as if such a
square meal hadn't come her way in days.

'Well,' she said, 'I'm just careful. I only cook once a week,
and make an enormous stewpot which lasts and lasts and
lasts.'

Into this pot went, apparently, everything that was in
season, and there was always pearl barley and kidney
beans to give it body if it seemed to be on the thin side.
Soya could also make it go further, but she wasn't too keen
on soya. She didn't feel in any sense that she was cheating
herself by being too economical, for she often ate fish and
meat, and the stewpot was always there to fill her up.
What made everything easier, in her opinion, was that she
had to write down every single expense, every tuppence-
worth of this or that, so that a complete list of outgoings
could be compiled and sent to the community bursar every
time she wanted more money. 'If you have to write it down,
then you know for sure how much things cost, and you
don't find yourself suddenly paying too much for
anything,' she said.

I don't know about everyone else but when I try and
write things down, say at the end of the day, I can only
remember about half the expenditures. I assume, therefore,
either villainy on someone else's part, or a hole in my pocket,
and cannot believe that I actually spent all the money
which seems to be missing. But what I can believe is that a
total record, kept religiously, is the only proper system for

knowing where it has all gone. And for knowing where it ought to go next week, with a bit more economy on certain items and therefore a bit more to spare for others.

Of course, as any student will tell you, the supermarkets must be watched like a hawk for any sudden downgrading of some commodity. Late on Saturday afternoon is a good time for snapping up damaged biscuits, dented tins, vegetables on their way out, and produce that isn't selling. My lunch-time companion, always happy to take advantage of such blessings, felt that a lot of spoiled or damaged food was jettisoned instead of being sold because that was often easier. If damaged tins were dumped on the poor it is just possible, isn't it, that a newspaper could make capital out of the issue – 'Giant Food Combine sells sub-standard produce to the needy'? It fits in with those stories about out-of-date drugs being marketed in the third world. Such a drug may be better than no drug at all to the impoverished sick, but the headlines don't make it seem that way.

Anyway, what else did my nun do to make ends meet? Well, she didn't have a fridge as she doesn't really see the need for one, save that milk in summer can go off on the few really hot days unless one takes care. And she pays for her gas heating via a meter, for in that way she is both more economical and is never astounded by some colossal bill. And she never uses public transport. That's far too expensive and her bike pays for itself over and over again, however many times tyres and tubes and lights have to be replaced. But above all, and quite the most important thing, was that business of writing everything down, every 10p for the gas, every pint of milk, every item from the shop. She said there were two quite different kinds of people in every supermarket, those who have only a vague idea how much the till total will come to and those who know precisely what the final sum will be. She was in this latter group, a smaller group by far. 'Don't the others mind how much things are going to cost?' she asked.

Which brought our conversation round to the nub of the matter. Are people really worse off these days and finding it harder to make ends meet? There is recession, and unemployment, and less government spending, and inflation, but there is also the assertion from economists, or rather from some economists, that we are still better off than we have ever been before. Whatever we feel, we are spending less, proportionately, on the three critical essentials, housing, fuel and food. They account now for 43 per cent of our total budget. The rest, the remaining 57 per cent, goes on everything else - clothes, alcohol, tobacco, transport, holidays, savings, and so on. More homes than ever before have television sets - 96%; more have telephones - 66%; more have cars - 60%; more have washing machines and refrigerators.

Well, that's what they say. But we can't dispute this unless we tot up the actual cost each week, each year, of where the money goes. How many of us really know how much the car costs, not just in petrol and insurance, but in parking fees (and parking fines), in deterioration, in light bulbs and oil? And do we really know how much goes past our teeth, so to speak, in meals, drink, sandwiches casually bought, chocolate, dining out. Perhaps it doesn't matter, or shouldn't matter, and it's tedious to be quite so financially obsessed - that's so long as there is still money in the pocket. But it undoubtedly does matter for those at the bottom end of the scale, for those who really run out before the week is at an end.

'So do the poor,' I asked of my nun, 'do they keep a good budget of where the money goes?'

'No, not many of them. In fact, they're quite the worst,' she replied. 'And that's the problem. They don't have much. So they don't care about it. They don't spend very wisely, and so they're worse off than they ought to be.'

In general, these poorest people, on whom she spends so much of her time, and energy, and devotion, get through many more pounds per week than she does. She says that she has more than enough to live on, and lives comfortably, and likes luxuries, and gets them from time to time. They say they have nothing like enough to live on, are displeased at their lot, and can't afford luxuries.

'So do they know how much you get,' I asked, 'and would they be amazed if you told them that all your living, except for the rent, costs less than £10 a week?'

'Well, I don't tell them exactly,' she said. 'But I think that much of our work is by example. And this rubs off. And they do learn. They see me eating a Mars Bar, which is my kind of luxury, and I think they think about that. But they don't keep lists, in the main, of what they spend. I wish they would, for I am sure that would help.'

We finished our meal, and the waiter added up his list of what we had consumed. It came, alas, to much more than it costs one nun to live for a week. Outside in the sunny street she got on her bike, and I climbed into a ton-and-a-half of steel, my car. I had enjoyed the meal, and felt I had learned a lot, about life, about economy, and where the money goes. Perhaps we should all have a meal with a nun from time to time. She would find it more interesting than a Mars Bar, and we would profit. Of that I am very sure.

Suicide

One of the joys and penalties for British authors whose books are also published in America is that they are invited over to take part in promotional tours. I am not certain of their worth, in helping the publisher to sell more books, but I know that the list of happenings lined up for the arriving author is very varied. At the end of one such tour I found myself about to take part in a live chat show that lasted on radio in New York from midnight to 4 a.m. I and a few other insomniacs were to discuss a book of mine under the chairmanship of a man known as Long John. Quite how many other insomniacs might be listening to our nocturnal ramblings I had no idea, and how many of them might even remember to buy the book thereafter I had even less idea, but we all assembled and began on the talking marathon.

Some 17 coffees after we had begun we got on to the subject of suicide, one of the chapters in my book about the body.

'Why,' said Long John, 'why don't we call up those good people who talk to potential suicides, pretend we are about to do ourselves in, and see what they have to say?'

I said 'Not live, and without warning the people beforehand. It isn't, well, ethical,' I added, falling back on a word we all fall back on when we haven't an argument prepared to back up our sentiments.

'Oh, I'm sure it's ethical,' said Long John, and he indicated to his secretary that she should fetch the Manhattan phone books.

I continued to object, and so did one or two others on the panel, but soon we were all deep in those directories looking up relevant numbers. One of us thought that 'Help' was the crucial word for all would-be suicides, and discovered some likely-looking entries, such as Help Line, Helpers of the Holy Souls Society, Helping Exterminating Company, Helping Hands Inc, and Helpmates. I can't remember which ones we opted for, but I do remember warming to the task as I realised that potential suicides would be just as troubled as they too thumbed through the phone books looking for help and guidance. Someone looked up murder, with the argument that suicide was murder of a kind. He found Murder Ink, which turned out to be an ink firm, and Murder Music Inc, which was a music firm. Under death we found Death Records, another music firm of a similarly sick nature, and under Suicide, we found two names, Suicide Prevention, and Suicide Prevention League. All of this, the fumbling, the searching for other entries, the exclamations of success, and of failure, it was all broadcast – live – into the New York air.

Eventually, we had quite a list of numbers, and Long John was ready to do his stuff, to ask for aid as if *he* had come to the end of his tether. For technical reasons he had to lie on the floor as the microphone cable was just long enough to meet the telephone at the end of its cable if the two instruments were also on the floor. I protested to Long John for a final time, but he by then was busy dialling.

'Let's hear how these good people go about their business,' he said as the number began to ring.

I don't know what any of us expected, but what we got was a click and then a soft voice:

'If you are in trouble, and would like help, would you please leave your name and number, and we'll call you back at 9.30 in the morning. Click. If you're in trouble and would like help ...'

'Huh,' said Long John, and 'huh,' said all of us, including me.

My reservations vanished at once. What kind of help was that to be confronted with an answering machine?

'Let's call another,' we *all* said, and so we did.

But this time the number just rang and rang, and we debated whether no answer whatsoever was even worse than an answering machine. Long John was now dialling a third number, and this time a voice replied. Plainly our prostrate chairman hadn't thought out what to say, and so was taken aback, but he compromised with a sort of groan.

'Ohhhh,' he said.

'I can hear that there is someone there,' said the kindly

female voice at the other end. 'If you would like to speak to me I will be happy to listen.'

'Ohhh,' said Long John yet again, still short on ideas of how a would-be suicide might actually speak.

'Are you in pain?' said the kindly voice. 'If so, shall I get a doctor for you? If not, would you like to tell me your trouble? I have as long as you want, but it probably would help if you could speak to me.'

This was all too much for Long John. Remember that it was all being broadcast and, even if she didn't know that, he did, and he was aware that she was making more sense than he was. So he confessed that he wasn't actually in trouble, but was pretending to be so that he, Long John, and all his listeners, could find out what happened when someone in trouble did call. At this point I expected her to explode at the abrupt manner in which she was told that her intimate little conversation was actually being broadcast. But she didn't explode, and merely proceeded to win yet another point.

'If you want to say that you are Long John,' she said, 'that's all right by me. But I know you're not because I listen to him every night when I'm not answering calls, and I know his voice as well as I know my own. But let's call you Long John if you want it that way.'

This was all much too much for our prone presenter. Losing points was one thing. Being told that you aren't who you are was something else, and he immediately tried to become himself even more so. But it's difficult exaggerating yourself, accentuating your own quirks of speech, and he was failing.

'Dammit,' he said, 'why not turn on your radio, and then you'll find out that I am who I am?'

But the thought of that happening terrified our sound engineer in the next room. He rushed in saying that if she turned it on the howl and feedback would generally blow the system, and would Long John tell her not to. So he ended, limply, by saying that she was a wonderful person doing a wonderful job and it was equally wonderful for him, Long John, to be able to speak to her. Down went the phone, and we then had a commercial break, but each one of us had been part horrified, part amused, and part inspired by the confrontation. Eventually we all went our separate ways at 4 am, but I have never forgotten that gentle, helpful, friendly voice trying to be comforting at the end of a phone.

Thus, it came as a bit of a shock when I read the other day that these helpful organisations don't seem to do much good. I appreciate that it's a kind of sacrilege to say so, in that we want to feel they are doing good, but the cold facts seem to indicate otherwise. For example, in a booklet published here a couple of months ago by the Office of Health Economics, evidence has been collated about the Samaritans, the principal and most famous organisation in Britain aimed at preventing suicide. In the booklet it is stated that the organisation may be effective in 'reducing suicide rates to some extent, but there is no way of proving this'. A book published last year called *Can Social Work Survive* states that 'neither formal nor informal social work has been shown to be effective in the prevention of suicide or attempted suicide'. It's like being told that lifeboatmen don't save lives or that boy scouts shouldn't help old ladies across the street.

What is particularly disarming is that the suicide rate for Britain has been going down of late just at a time when the Samaritans have been building themselves up. The organisation began in 1953, modestly at first, but it expanded considerably during the 1960s. As if to reflect this increase in concern for those wishing to destroy themselves, the suicide rate in this country began to drop as from 1963. And it continued to drop fairly steadily thereafter. What could be easier, therefore, than to put the two facts together, the greater number of people at the end of a telephone and the gradual reduction in the suicide rate. The drop was extremely significant, in that the official total fell from about 5,500 a year in the mid-sixties to about 3,500 in the mid-seventies. What made it even more interesting was the extra fact that this certainly wasn't the case in the rest of Europe. No one else had the kind of drop that we experienced.

To begin with, even scientific work was able to associate the drop in suicides with the rise in the number of suicide prevention centres. Comparisons were made between

pairs of similar towns which were dissimilar only in that
one had a prevention centre and the other did not. Those
with centres experienced a drop in the suicide rate, and
those without experienced a rise. The results were, as
scientists phrase it, statistically significant. But, alas for
the conclusion, the results have since been challenged. For
example, the pairing of similar towns has been shown to
be more difficult than was at first supposed. Towns may
seem to be alike, but they are always different in all sorts
of ways. Like is, therefore, not being compared with like.
Also having a suicide prevention centre in a nearby town
may be influencing the suicide rate in that other town. In
other words, it isn't easy proving that suicide centres do
stop suicides, and it was the man who made the first study,
the one which seemed to forge a link between suicide
centres and a drop in suicides, who concluded in 1977 that
'Samaritans may be effective in reducing suicide rates to
some extent, but there is no way of proving this'.

What has undoubtedly done good since the 1960s is that
we no longer, in general, have such a toxic gas piped into
so many of our homes, and our doctors aren't prescribing
such quantities of barbiturates for us. On the subject of
gas I have always been amazed that something as
poisonous and as explosive as coal gas ever found its way
into our homes, but the gas we now use is far less lethal. As
a result the number of self-poisonings by gas is far
less than it used to be. On the subject of drugs, it is,
unfortunately, very easy to kill oneself with barbiturates,
and many people do so. It is very difficult to kill oneself
with many of the different pills being prescribed in much
greater numbers today; but, even so, an overdose of
something heads the current list of all suicide causes, the
Number One placing that used to be held by gas.

What has made those in the prevention business much
more concerned about suicide recently is that the rate is
now going up again. It was very comforting during the
1960s and early 70s when it was going down, but since
1975 it has in general been going up. And it has been doing
so despite the decrease in barbiturate prescription, despite
the falling toxicity of domestic gas, despite the better
hospital treatment for attempted suicides, and despite the

rise in the welfare agencies. We are in a recession, as we all know, and it is interesting to see that the last big suicide peak was in 1933 when there were 2,800,000 out of work.

It has now been estimated that a fifth of all acute medical admissions to hospitals are as a result of deliberate self-harm, and this trend is increasing. We are killing ourselves at about the rate that we kill ourselves on the roads, but the road deaths receive tremendous attention and research and finance in our efforts to cut down that slaughter. The suicide problem receives far less finance, far less research, and far less attention. So I think it was absolutely right that night in New York, for Long John to lie on the floor and call up those agencies to find out a little of what goes on.

Nuclear War

The other day a student told me that she wasn't interested in feminism because it distracted from the real priorities. In her case these amounted to the need for revolution and, once that had happened, all the various minor issues – such as feminism – could be dealt with expeditiously. In a sense, in a considerable sense, she has a point. If the minor issues will all be satisfactorily tackled as soon as the major issue has been concluded, let's forget about them for the time being and concentrate upon it.

'Feminism,' she said, 'is a waste of effort. Only revolution matters.'

It so happens that this is the last talk in yet another series of *Sideways Looks* and, with her strident words still ringing in our ears, I propose to look back upon some of the subjects covered, and what you – dear listeners – had to say about them. Is it right, in short, to reflect upon minor issues, or should you, and I, be most concerned with the major ones? Your letters, after all, reflect your concern about a subject in which I have been concerned, and so provide a guideline, a response like the buzz of an audience when some lecturer hits a sympathetic chord. So what did you buzz most loudly about?

Well, the talks were, in my opinion, fairly wide-ranging. A short while after each programme the letters came in, and to very varying degrees. No one seemed to care much about suicide, that particular form of scythe which takes almost as many deaths as do our roads. As for nuns, I got letters from some other nuns, which was nice, and even received one doll nun, which was nicer still. Some people said that they too live on less than £10 a week and so what was special about nuns, save I suppose that nuns choose to do so. But my greatest sin was in daring to mention the British dog. That brought more letters than nuns, suicide, and everything else, and leaves me more amazed than ever at our priorities. What is there about this one animal, or rather the five million who live with us, that causes such vitriol?

What I had advocated, before we lose track of the argument and become enmeshed in all the snapping and snarling that went on, was that dogs should be better controlled. As pains for expressing this opinion, I was told that it was 'a miserable lot of drivel', that dogs only dislike and bite people when there is something wrong with those people, that I plainly disliked dogs, that dogs are much nicer than my friends are, that the talk was a complete flop, the sooner I was made redundant the better, and I and my kind were obviously busy collecting enough atomic weapons to wipe everything out.

Remember what I was advocating was a £5 dog licence for the better control of dogs. I wasn't for hanging and quartering the animals, or suggesting they shouldn't eat meat, and heaven knows what would have happened had I advocated these things. Presumably I would have been hung and drawn myself by those most dogged humans of them all, namely those who rise up in anger and in their thousands whenever the remotest suggestion is made that the total freedom at present enjoyed by the dog population should be modestly curtailed.

Anyway, I am happy to report that not all the letters were from the extreme right wing of the dog world. About 80 per cent welcomed the talk and wrote to say so because, in their opinion, I would be inundated with the other kind of letter, and each of them wished, in part, to redress the balance. So, bearing that 80 per cent in mind, the tide of apathy about free-ranging and free-biting dogs may be turning. Perhaps it is now time that they too should have their freedoms clipped so that they come more into line with the rest of us. Incidentally, I did find it odd that the 80 per cent praised the talk whereas the 20 per cent who were against it attacked me rather than the talk.

'It is not dogs that threaten the world,' proclaimed one correspondent. 'But humans like you.'

Which brings me to my main concern. Why worry about dogs, or nuns, or anything else, when there is the greatest worry of all still, so to speak, at large? Like the girl who dismissed feminism because of the greater issue of world revolution, why worry about dog failings when there is the greater concern of human failure leading, at its most extreme form, to nuclear war? Don't all other worries pale beside that one, and, therefore, shouldn't that one be our prime concern at all times? Why care about anything that isn't directly concerned with the total threat to life on earth?

It isn't true that we have been living with this threat ever since Hiroshima and Nagasaki were atomically destroyed in 1945. At that time, despite their bluff pronouncements to the contrary, the Americans had no more nuclear weapons up their sleeves. It had taken considerable effort to manufacture enough plutonium and refine enough uranium for those two and, with their detonation, that temporarily exhausted their available supplies. It was fortunate that the Americans did not have a third bomb to press home their demand for surrender even more aggressively, and it was also fortunate that the Japanese surrendered. However, there have been 36 years since then and, according to the *Bulletin of Atomic Scientists*, there are now 40,000 nuclear devices of one kind or another in existence. They are of varying size, sophistication and destructiveness and all of them are more advanced, if that's the right word, than the primitive devices dropped on Japan in August 1945.

So, in remembering the weapons now in existence, it's important to remember just what a primitive atomic weapon can do. And did do. At Hiroshima 75,000 people were killed, and another 100,000 injured, out of the total city population of 245,000. From the medical point of view, which becomes dominant when 100,000 are injured, there were 30 doctors left out of the 150 formerly in existence, and there were 126 nurses remaining out of 1,780. It is for this sort of reason that the medical profession has of late – and only of late – been concerning itself not so much with what to do should another bomb drop but how to prevent one ever being dropped. In March of this year was the first-ever formal gathering of the body known as International Physicians for the Prevention of Nuclear War. Although this assembled in Virginia, USA, there were 14 doctors from the Soviet Union among the delegates, and the basic message at the meeting's end was that, as in all else, prevention is better than cure.

The doctors have been trying to observe the arms race in a rational manner. For example, they have evaluated what might happen should just two bombs land in the Boston area of Massachusetts with its population of three million people. Over a million of them would be killed outright, and another million would die later. Of the 6,500 doctors about 10 per cent would be able to do a pathetic job in looking after the sick. That's if just two bombs were dropped on one area but, as I've said, there are 40,000 around the world. The threat they pose is out of all proportion to every other foreseeable kind of tragedy. A total disruption of all food supplies would not be so bad as the firing of those 40,000. The liberation of a new plague, equivalent in its venom to the Black Death, would not be so bad because that only killed one-third of the city people, but nuclear bombs can kill and kill for years thereafter as the fall-out falls and the various radio-active isotopes live out their ionizing lives. A nuclear war has been called 'the last epidemic' and rightly so for there wouldn't be any others. It's heads we lose, tails we lose, and anyone who speaks of a contained nuclear war, or the sensible use of tactical nuclear weapons, is – in my opinion – short on knowledge that all wars escalate. Or, to quote Professor George Kistiakowsky, former head of the explosives division of the Manhattan Project that built the first atomic bomb: 'It will be a miracle if no nuclear warheads are exploded in anger before the end of this century, and only a slightly smaller miracle if this doesn't lead to a nuclear holocaust'.

Not many of us, I fear, believe in miracles, and not many of us have much faith in all our fellow human beings. Five countries are now known to possess nuclear weapons, and perhaps India has them, and probably Israel and South Africa, and certainly that list will grow. I wonder which countries in the world we would least like to have nuclear weapons; those with most to lose, or those with least to lose.

I have not touched on this topic before in these talks, this greatest and most awful topic of them all, and I wonder if or when I shall do so again. The world will have gone mad

if it, or rather if a part of it, decides to destroy itself and all
the rest of us simultaneously. So perhaps it's best if we just
strive for sanity and settle for that. And how can we best
keep sane other than by worrying about the smaller things,
our individual problems, our homes, our microscopic jobs,
our pathetic personal influence upon the global scene?

And maybe that is why we're quite so dotty about dogs. I
have never had such a mailbag as when talking about
them. The letters, in part, may have made me despair, as
they yapped verbally at my throat, but better by far this
kind of onslaught than any other kind. In fact, there is a
curious kind of rule that the lesser the subject the greater
the discussion and interest that it provokes, as with
Northcote Parkinson's committee spending all day dis-
cussing the new bicycle shed and then abruptly rubber-
stamping proposals for a new power station. We can grasp
bike sheds more easily than power stations, and can rage
about the turd world – as I'm afraid I called it – of the dogs
rather than the third world with all its hunger and
despair. I doubted the sanity of some of the letter writers
but, if the biggest issues are too big for us to contemplate,
then it must be right to interest ourselves, however insanely, in the lesser ones, and in the least of all – such as dogs.

So, let's, as a final word, return to them. I ended last time
with a brief reference to the couple whose Dobermann
Pinschers had run wild in Erith, Kent, and had attacked 11
people in 10 minutes. Several facts emerged from that little
incident. The first was that one of the dogs had already
attacked a human, and its owner was then fined £10. Not
much, you might say, but did you know that the maximum
fine for *inciting* your dog to attack another human is £20?
That's not much either, and could be worth it on occasion.
Also one of the people who was attacked died three days
later, and the pathologist said it was beyond reasonable
doubt that the victim's heart attack was triggered off by the
shock of the dog's attack. So I wonder what will happen to
that dog owner should the Director of Public Prosecutions
decide to bring a charge? In this country who knows? Another little fine? Certainly the case should keep us all chatting
like mad, and at least will stop us thinking about nuclear
war and what will happen if that is ever triggered off.